SEARCHING FOR
SAPPHO

SEARCHING FOR
SAPPHO

The Lost Songs and World of the First Woman Poet

Including new translations of all of
Sappho's surviving poetry

PHILIP FREEMAN

W. W. NORTON & COMPANY
Independent Publishers Since 1923
New York · London

For information about permission to reproduce selections from this book,
write to Permissions, W. W. Norton & Company, Inc.,
500 Fifth Avenue, New York, NY 10110

For information about special discounts for bulk purchases, please
contact W. W. Norton Special Sales at specialsales@wwnorton.com
or 800-233-4830

Manufacturing by RR Donnelley North Harrisonburg
Book design by Ellen Cipriano
Production manager: Louise Mattarelliano

Library of Congress Cataloging-in-Publication Data

Names: Freeman, Philip, 1961– author. | Sappho. Works. English. 2016.
Title: Searching for Sappho : the lost songs and world of the
first woman poet : including new translations of all of Sappho's
surviving poetry /Philip Freeman.
Description: New York ; London : W.W. Norton & Company, 2016. |
Includes bibliographical references and index.
Identifiers: LCCN 2015039760 | ISBN 9780393242232 (hardcover)
Subjects: LCSH: Sappho. | Greek poetry—History and criticism.
Classification: LCC PA4409 .F74 2015 | DDC 884/.01—dc23 LC record
available at http://lccn.loc.gov/2015039760

W. W. Norton & Company, Inc.
500 Fifth Avenue, New York, N.Y. 10110
www.wwnorton.com

W. W. Norton & Company Ltd.
Castle House, 75/76 Wells Street, London W1T 3QT

1 2 3 4 5 6 7 8 9 0

*For my
mother,
wife,
and
daughter*

CONTENTS

INTRODUCTION / xi

MAP / xxv

TIMELINE / xxvii

1. Childhood / 1

2. Wedding Songs / 23

3. A Mother's Love / 57

4. Family Matters / 85

5. Loving Women / 109

6. The Goddess / 133

7. Unyielding Time / 149

EPILOGUE / 161

THE POEMS OF SAPPHO / 173

ACKNOWLEDGMENTS / 239

NOTES / 241

FURTHER READING / 277

INDEX / 285

INTRODUCTION

SAPPHO: Daughter of Simon or Eumenos or Eerigyios or Ecrytos or Semos or Camon or Etarchos or Scamandronymos. Her mother was named Cleis. She was a woman of the island of Lesbos, from the town of Eresus, and was a poet of the lyre. She flourished during the 42nd Olympic games, when Alcaeus, Stesichorus, and Pittacus were also living. Her three brothers were Larichus, Charaxus, and Erygius. She was married to a very wealthy man named Cerylas who traded from the island of Andros. Her daughter by him was named Cleis. She had three companions and friends named Atthis, Telesippa, and Megara, but her relations with them earned her a shameful reputation. Her pupils were Anagora of Miletus, Gongyla of Colophon, and Eunica of Salamis. She composed nine books of lyric songs and invented the plectrum. She also composed epigrams, elegiac verse, iambic poetry, and solo songs.

— *SUDA* ENCYCLOPEDIA (TENTH CENTURY AD)

NOTHING EXCITING HAD happened in the Egyptian village of el-Behnesa for over a thousand years.

In ancient times it had been known as Oxyrhynchus—"the city of the sharp-nosed fish." In those days it had been a prosperous regional capital on a branch of the Nile with streets full of government bureaucrats and retired Roman army officers. Temples to the ancient gods of Egypt and newly built Christian churches stood side by side. Brothels and bathhouses shared the town with monasteries and private homes boasting beautiful gardens. Palm trees lined the colonnaded avenues, the bustling central square hosted caravans and merchants from lands beyond the western desert, and a beautiful open-air theater held thousands of cheering spectators. But with the fall of Rome and the decline of classical civilization, the city had withered away to a squalid collection of mud huts. The limestone blocks of the ancient town had gradually been carted off to build barns or burned to make fertilizer for the fields. All that was left of the city's former glory was a single Roman column rising from the dust on the edge of town.

But on a warm winter's day in 1896, the villagers of el-Behnesa witnessed a strange sight as two young men dressed in foreign clothes appeared in their town armed with shovels and baskets. For three weeks the men dug in the ancient cemetery with little to show for their efforts, but then they asked the local farmers and goatherds if they had ever found anything interesting in the garbage dump of the old city. The villagers shook their heads and told the strangers there was nothing of value there, only bits of ancient papyrus. That was exactly what the visitors wanted to hear.

Bernard Grenfell and Arthur Hunt had studied at Oxford University and climbed together in the Alps during their vacations. They were students of the new science of archaeology and had come to the forgotten city of Oxyrhynchus to look not for gold or treasure, but for written documents from another time. Papyrus, made from a reed that grew on the banks of the Nile, was the common writing material of the ancient world, and under the right conditions—buried in a bone-dry, oxygen-poor environment in the desert—it could survive for centuries.

The British explorers settled into a canvas tent and hired every man and boy they could find to help them dig. They did not expect to unearth much of interest at the dump of el-Behnesa,

A. S. Hunt and B. P. Grenfell at the Fayûm in Egypt c. 1900.
(COURTESY OF THE EGYPT EXPLORATION SOCIETY
AND IMAGING PROJECT, OXFORD)

Egyptian workers digging for papyrus fragments
at Oxyrhynchus, Egypt.

(COURTESY OF THE EGYPT EXPLORATION SOCIETY
AND IMAGING PROJECT, OXFORD)

but they soon came across a piece of ancient papyrus with writing on it. Back in their tent that night, they carefully placed the fragile document beneath the light of a lamp and began to read the faded Greek letters:

> *And Jesus said, "I stood in the middle of the world and in the flesh was seen by them, but I found everyone drunk and no one thirsty."*

These lines were recorded in none of the Christian gospels but were something entirely new—a collection of previously unknown sayings attributed to Jesus himself.

Electrified by their discovery, Grenfell and Hunt threw themselves into their work. Over the next few months they found so many papyrus fragments that they had to use biscuit tins and boxes made from old kerosene containers to store the precious writings for transport back to Oxford. Many of the fragments told stories of daily life, such as the tale of a father who broke off his daughter's engagement to a young man because of the man's immoral behavior or a receipt for the sale of a female slave. Some were tax records, personal letters, or arrest warrants, and one was the monthly meat bill for a cook.

But the prize of Grenfell and Hunt's first year of excavation was a small piece of papyrus that neither of them—indeed no one in the world—had ever expected to see. On the fragile remains were just a few lines of poetry written in ancient Greek:

> *. . . Nereids, grant that*
> *my brother come back to me unharmed*
> *and that all he wishes for in his heart*
> > *comes true.*

> *And grant that he atone for all his past mistakes.*
> *Make him a joy to his friends and a grief*
> *to his enemies. And may no one bring us sorrow*
> > *ever again.*

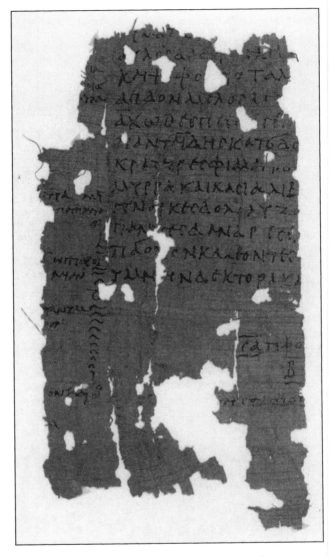

Papyrus fragment from Oxyrhynchus, Egypt
(Oxyrhynchus papyrus 2076), with Sappho Poem 44.

There was no mistaking the archaic language, style, or poetic meter of the verses. They belonged to the first woman poet, indeed the first woman writer known to literary history, whose songs until that day had survived only through a few scattered quotations in later Greek and Roman authors. What Grenfell and Hunt had found was a previously unknown poem composed by none other than Sappho of Lesbos.

The two archaeologists could not believe their eyes. In the publication of that year's papyri, they told of their discovery and lamented that it was surely a once-in-a-lifetime event: "It is not very likely that we shall find another poem of Sappho."

But it was only the beginning.

WHO WAS SAPPHO, this woman who stands at the beginning of history and still so enchants modern readers? The facts about her life are few and often subject to dispute, but from her own poetry and the scattered comments about her in ancient authors, we know that she was born on the isle of Lesbos in the Aegean Sea sometime in the latter part of the seventh century BC, a time of tremendous intellectual, social, and commercial change in the Greek world. There, she was part of a wealthy aristocratic family that vied for political control of her prosperous and cosmopolitan island. She was married and the mother of a much-beloved daughter. She endured exile in Sicily at some point during her adult life but presumably returned to Lesbos after a time, where she died an old woman.

We also know that Sappho wrote some of the most beautiful poems ever composed. Some of these "songs"—for they were meant to be sung to the accompaniment of a lyre—were for public performances; others were private compositions. Most of her poems are songs of love wholly unlike the epics of Homer, who lived in the century before her. Gone are the blood and glory of the Trojan War and the monster-battling adventures of Odysseus. Instead, the verses of Sappho are deeply personal and celebrate the joys and agony of the human heart:

> *When I look at you even for a moment*
> *I can no longer speak.*

> *My tongue fails and a subtle*
> *fire races beneath my skin,*
> *I see nothing with my eyes*
> *and my ears hum.*

> *Sweat pours from me and a trembling*
> *seizes my whole body. I am greener*
> *than grass and it seems I am little short*
> *of dying.*

Others of her songs call down curses on a rival or make bawdy jokes about a bridegroom's giant erection. But whatever the subject, Sappho's poems are always delightful and woven as intricately and beautifully as the finest Lydian cloth.

Although ancient writers say her poetry once filled nine scrolls in the ancient Library of Alexandria, only a few remnants have survived the centuries. Of these, scarcely a handful come close to being complete poems. Many have missing words or lines, represented by an ellipsis (. . .) in the text. Often nothing remains except for a single line or even a solitary word. And yet, what has survived of Sappho's verses reveals her as one of the greatest poets of antiquity, if not of all time.

Searching for Sappho is a story of discovery, not only of the physical remains of Sappho's poems, but, as much as possible, of the woman herself and her world. The poetry of Sappho gives us the rarest of gifts—a genuine woman's voice from an age overwhelmingly dominated by men. Thus, a major goal of this book is to use her songs as a window into the lives of all women in the classical world and to learn what the different stages of a woman's life were like in ancient Greece. What was it like to be a young girl over two thousand years ago? Why were marriage and motherhood at the center of a woman's life? How did life change as a woman grew older in classical times? The similarities between the lives of ancient and modern women are surprising, but the differences can be astonishing.

Not all of Sappho's poems come from ancient papyri discovered in Egypt. More than half of the two hundred or so poems and fragments of Sappho have survived the centuries as quotations in the works of often obscure ancient authors, such as the grammarian Apollonius Dyscolus. Most of these men—they were all male writers—passed on only a line or two, but a few included passages long enough to give readers through the centuries an appreciation of Sappho's skill at crafting a poem as a whole. One such song, of seven full stanzas, is a prayer to Aphrodite embedded in an otherwise dry book on literary composition by the Greek critic Dionysius of Halicarnassus, who lived five hundred years after Sappho. The first stanza sets the stage for something quite remarkable that follows:

> *Deathless Aphrodite on your dazzling throne,*
> *child of Zeus, weaver of snares, I pray to you,*
> *do not, with anguish and pain, O Lady,*
>   *break my heart.*

Many of the shorter quotations of Sappho in ancient authors' texts were used simply to illustrate a particular point of grammar or style, but a few longer passages continued to be quoted until the twelfth century. The last surviving copy of Sappho's poems may have burned soon after in the fires that ravaged Constantinople during the Fourth Crusade, but whatever the fate of her writings, there were no new poems of Sappho for the world to admire until modern times.

In the twentieth century, archaeologists, beginning with Grenfell and Hunt at Oxyrhynchus, uncovered enough fragments of Sappho's poetry on papyrus, pottery, and mummy wrappings that we can begin to appreciate the scope of her talent. And the discoveries continue, with a new and almost complete poem of Sappho revealed to the world as recently as 2014 after lying undiscovered for decades in a university library in Mississippi. The little-known story of the recovery of many of Sappho's works reads like a detective novel with idealistic young adventurers, shady antiquities dealers, and fragments of poetry hidden away in the most unlikely places. But it's also the more prosaic but no less intriguing story of painstaking research by scholars, men and women alike, who have labored for decades and labor still to piece together her poems.

No one can write a true biography of Sappho, since we know so little for certain about her life. Of the testimony about her that we do have from the Greek and Roman world, much is of questionable veracity, if not plainly fanciful or unfairly hostile. Many male writers in ancient times could not bear the thought of a woman having such talent. Since her later critics couldn't dispute her gift for poetry, they turned instead to slander, claiming she was not a proper woman at all. She was called a prostitute and mocked on stage as immoral. And in a world where males prized a woman's fair skin and well-shaped form second only to her modesty, she was described as short, dark, and ugly, even though the earliest portraits of her on vases portray a beautiful woman.

When it comes to Sappho, arguing from silence is a dangerous business. That is, speculating about Sappho's life from what she *doesn't* say in her poetry can lead us to very uncertain conclusions, especially since so few of her poems have survived the ages. But if Sappho's poetry can't tell us everything we would like to know, and if the ancient authors are sometimes less than reliable, where can we turn to create an accurate picture of her life? In some ways such a quest is impossible, but we needn't despair if we keep as our goal not a biography, but an image of her life framed by details gleaned from her poetry. And if we look beyond her poems to other sources from the ancient world—literary, artistic, and archaeological—we can create a plausible, if partial, picture of what Sappho's life must have been like. Many of these ancient sources come from several centuries after Sappho, and quite a few are from Athens, the one city in ancient Greece we know a good deal about. But the life of a woman in fifth-century-BC Athens was similar enough to that of a Greek woman on the island of Lesbos two hundred years earlier to provide us with important insights into Sappho's life.

Just as the ancient sources can help us understand Sappho, her poetry can, in turn, reveal much about the lives of other women in the classical world. Almost everything written in ancient times, from Homer to Saint Augustine, was composed by men. Even on those occasions when male Greek and Roman authors bothered to write about women, the words come to us from a male point of view, often full of ignorance and prejudice. But Sappho opens a window into her own life and the lives of all women from ancient times, giving them their first and best voice from long ago.

One final question that should be addressed is the controversial nature of Sappho's sexuality. Sappho was a native of the island of Lesbos, but was she a lesbian—a lover of women—in the modern sense of the word? In spite of many efforts over the years to portray her otherwise, the evidence we have strongly suggests that she indeed had sexual relationships with other women. But a major problem in understanding Sappho's sexuality is that modern categories of sexual preference and orientation mean little in the ancient world. Acceptable sexual behavior varied greatly by time, place, social class, and other factors in early Greece, but in general, adult men were free to have intimate relations with members of either gender, as long as they fulfilled their duty to family and community by marrying and fathering children. We know much less about Greek women, but it's clear from ancient (male) writers that throughout most of the Greek and Roman world, there was less tolerance for same-sex relationships among females. Yet Sappho often claims in her poetry to love other women and writes openly about the passion she feels for them:

> *And on a soft bed*
> *delicate . . .*
> *you let loose your desire.*

and

> *. . . for when I see you face to face*
> *. . . even Hermione*
> *. . . to compare you to golden-haired Helen*
> *. . . among mortal women, know this*
> *. . . you could free me from all my cares*
> *. . . on the riverbanks*
> *. . . all through the night*

Some scholars have suggested that the songs Sappho composed did not reflect her own life but were a poetic fiction, a persona. While Sappho undoubtedly at times writes in the voice of another, most of her poems are so deeply personal that it begs credibility to argue that she was merely using poetic license to present herself as something she wasn't. If Sappho wasn't in fact a lover of women, she did an excellent job of pretending to be.

Many admirable volumes on Sappho have been written by scholars for scholars, but this is a book for everyone else. I assume no special knowledge of classical history among readers and certainly no training in ancient Greek, only a desire to learn more about one of the greatest writers who ever lived and her world. For in the end, Sappho is a poet for everyone. Anyone who has ever been in love or known the sorrow of loss or felt the years slipping away all too quickly can find their own lives in her immortal songs.

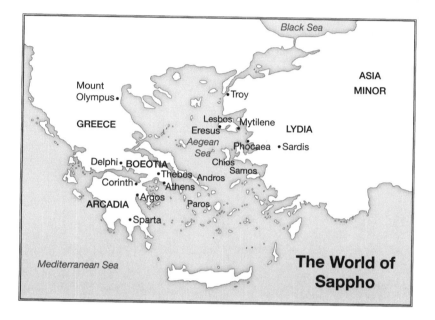

The World of Sappho

TIMELINE

BC	
750–700	Homer composes the *Iliad* and the *Odyssey*.
late 7th–early 6th centuries	Life of Sappho.
3rd century	Oldest surviving fragments of Sappho are written on potsherd and papyrus.
1st century	Catullus, Horace, and other Roman poets are influenced by Sappho; Dionysius of Halicarnassus records Sappho Poem 1.
AD	
1st–3rd centuries	Citizens of Lesbos feature Sappho on their coins.
2nd century	Maximus of Tyre lectures on Sappho in Rome; Hephaestion preserves many fragments of Sappho's poetry.
2nd–3rd centuries	Most surviving Oxyrhynchus papyri of Sappho are written.
c. 362	Roman emperor Julian quotes Sappho.
7th century	Sappho's poetry is written on parchment in Egypt.
12th century	Byzantine scholar and bishop Eustathius quotes last Sappho poem from antiquity.
1897	Grenfell and Hunt discover first Sappho papyrus at Oxyrhynchus.
2005	Sappho's newly discovered poem on growing older is published.
2014	"The Brothers Poem" is published.

SEARCHING FOR
SAPPHO

1

CHILDHOOD

*Don't worry if the others return while I remain here in
Alexandria. . . . If you give birth to a living child. If it's a boy,
let it live. If it's a girl, leave it to die.*

— LETTER FROM A MAN TO HIS WIFE (1ST CENTURY BC)

WE KNOW LESS about Sappho's childhood than about
any other part of her life. Because she rarely mentions
her early years in her surviving poetry, we must rely on other
ancient sources to imagine what life was like for a girl growing
up on Lesbos in the seventh century BC. Many of these sources
date from centuries later and from elsewhere in Greece, so they
must be used with caution. Just because Athenian girls dressed
as bears and worshipped Artemis in a coming-of-age festival
doesn't mean Sappho and her friends did as well. We can learn
something of Sappho's childhood from the hints she gives us in
her poems and from the limited testimony about her early years
in classical authors, but the best we can hope for is to create a
tentative picture of her life as a girl by looking at the lives of other
young women in ancient Greece.

The greatest challenge in the ancient world for children, especially girls, was survival. Disease, poverty, and a widespread preference for sons over daughters all took their toll. Infant mortality is notoriously difficult to establish in ancient times, but the best estimates are that one out of every four or even three children never saw their first birthday. There was no modern sanitation in the birthing room, and difficult deliveries were often a death sentence for both mother and child.

We know from Sappho's poems that she came from a wealthy merchant family. A baby's chances of living were undoubtedly better among such families, who could afford the best medical care, primitive though it was, and enough food for a nursing mother. But rich or poor, just as a woman weaned one child, another would be on its way. More often than not, a Greek woman from her midteens until well into her forties was pregnant.

Even if a child survived the trauma of birth, there was no guarantee the father would allow it to live. Classical stories are full of infants such as the newborn Oedipus or Romulus and Remus left to die in the empty countryside. But exposure was not just a literary motif. The Greeks called it *ekthesis* or "putting outside"—a pleasant euphemism for a most unpleasant act. Whether because of the inability of a family to feed a child, questionable paternity, birth defects, or other reasons, a father could choose to leave a child to die in the forest, on a dung heap, or in a place where it might be found by someone who would adopt it. In Sparta, the city elders examined all infants to decide those worthy to live, and those who failed the test were thrown into a pit on a nearby mountain.

To the ancient Greeks, exposure was not infanticide, since the child was not killed outright but had its fate placed in the hands of the gods. In this way of thinking the parents could avoid the bloodguilt that came with murder. Sometimes an exposed baby would be rescued by those who couldn't have their own child or by slave merchants, but most infants were probably left unclaimed. Some cities, such as Thebes and Ephesus, outlawed the practice, while others tried to regulate it. Males were more valued than females for economic reasons in a world where parents relied on sons to provide labor and to care for them in their later years, so it's likely that more girls were left to die than boys. The ancient Greek comedy writer Posidippus was undoubtedly exaggerating, but there must have been some truth in his grim humor: "If you have a son you raise him, even if you're poor. If you have a daughter you expose her, even if you're rich." We have no idea how common the practice was on Lesbos, but it's likely that on the day Sappho was born into a world of comfort and welcome, the cries of abandoned baby girls were fading into silence somewhere on the island.

MALE OR FEMALE, a child was not a member of its family until being accepted into the household during a formal ceremony. In Athens this was called the *Amphidromia* ("running around") and took place a few days after the child's birth. At this celebration the infant was given a name and carried at a trot around the family hearth, the sacred center of the home. Joyful feasting followed with a wide assortment of foods including, according to one ancient source, toasted cheese, boiled cabbages covered with olive oil, baked lamb, tenderized octopus tentacles, and many bowls of wine.

Soon after this, boys in Athens were publicly enrolled during their first year into their fathers' phratries, or fraternal organizations, but the public rituals of baby girls in ancient Greece are less well known. One hint comes from a late classical text, which records that, in Athens at least, it was customary to place a tuft of wool—a symbol of her future role in weaving—on the door of a household with a newborn baby girl. Another clue comes from a recently discovered image in stone found in northern Greece at Echinos. On the relief is a carving of a woman presenting an infant girl to Artemis, a virgin goddess praised by Sappho who was honored by women for her help in childbirth and as a guardian of young girls. In front of the infant, at the center of the stone, is an animal ready for sacrifice. Behind the baby is a servant carrying fruit and cakes on her head. At the rear is a veiled woman, probably the mother, bearing a bowl of incense in thanksgiving to the goddess for a successful birth and as a prayer seeking a blessing for her new daughter.

SAPPHO'S MOTHER WAS Cleis, a name the poet would later give to her own daughter. Girls were usually named for a family member, often a parent's mother, so Sappho may have taken her own name from her grandmother. We know little of the woman who bore Sappho, since Sappho mentions her mother only once in her surviving songs:

For my mother used to say
that when she was young it was
a great ornament if someone had her hair
bound in a purple headband.

Sappho never mentions her father. Later writers list no fewer than eight possible names for him, though the oldest and most common is Scamandronymos, a name with epic echoes, as it derives from the Scamander River that flowed past Troy. According to a late tradition found in the Roman poet Ovid, Sappho's father died when she was only a child:

Six birthdays had passed for me when I gathered the bones
   of my father,
dead before his time, and let them drink my tears.

This may be nothing but a literary fiction, but Ovid had access to poems of Sappho now lost to us in which she may have written of losing her father as a child. If there is any truth to the story, Sappho grew up in a volatile and dangerous world without him.

Sappho never discusses any sisters in her poems, but ancient writers and the poet herself record that she had three brothers, named Erygius, Larichus, and Charaxus. The eldest may have been Erygius, but Larichus was apparently the youngest and Sappho's favorite. He would later rise to the high position of cup-bearer at the Mytilene town hall. Sappho would one day write scathing satires against her third brother, Charaxus, for sullying the family name with a prostitute in Egypt.

Sappho's birthplace and home for most of her life was the beautiful island of Lesbos in the northern Aegean Sea. It lies just a few miles off the coast of Asia Minor (modern Turkey), which is clearly visible across the strait separating Lesbos from the mainland. The island itself is quite large but is divided now, as it was in antiquity, by two bays that reach deep into its interior. In Sappho's day it was covered with pine forests and steep valleys with cultivated olive groves and apple trees. Even today it is a major flyway for birds migrating between Europe and Africa. Flowers grow everywhere on the warm and verdant island, while soaring mountains catch the cool afternoon breezes blowing from the north in the summer.

We know that Sappho was born on Lesbos, but where on the island is uncertain. The most likely place is Eresus, a small town on the southwestern coast now in ruins. But some claim she was from the opposite side of the island, at Mytilene, the major city of Lesbos in ancient times, as today. Sappho herself doesn't say, but one likely possibility is that she was indeed born in Eresus and moved to Mytilene later, perhaps when she married.

The year of Sappho's birth is another thorny problem. Ancient writers say she lived at the same time as Alcaeus, another poet of Lesbos, and Pittacus, who ruled the island, as well as Alyattes, the king of nearby Lydia. All three of these men lived in the years just before and after 600 BC. We know that Sappho went into exile in Sicily sometime before 595 BC, so a reasonable guess is that she was born in the late seventh century BC and died some decades later.

Whatever the exact year of her birth, Sappho lived during a revolutionary period of Greek history. Sappho's time was christened the "Archaic period" by modern historians who saw it as a precursor to the golden age of Greece in the fifth century BC, but the term is misleading. The long centuries of decline and struggle since the collapse of the mighty Bronze Age kingdoms of Greece had at last come to an end in the century before Sappho. Populations were exploding across the Aegean world, and trade was flourishing. Greek cities were establishing colonies on the coasts of the Black Sea, Africa, Italy, and even the distant shores of Gaul and Spain. Phoenician traders from the Near East were filling the markets of Greek cities with exotic goods and had brought with them an alphabet from which the Greeks forged their own writing system. The first philosophers and scientists in Western history, such as Thales of nearby Miletus, were beginning to speculate about the nature and origin of the universe.

And it was an age of poetry. In the previous century the bard Homer, traditionally thought to be from the island of Chios just to the south of Lesbos, had shaped the stories of Achilles and Odysseus into the *Iliad* and the *Odyssey*. His contemporary, the poet Hesiod, had composed songs about of the birth of the gods and how Zeus had devised the ultimate punishment for men: the beautiful Pandora, ancestor of all mortal women. And just a few years before Sappho's birth, the poet Archilochus from the island of Paros had begun to sing of decidedly nonheroic themes, such as throwing away his shield and fleeing from a battle.

. . .

DAILY LIFE FOR a growing child in Sappho's time in many ways wasn't so different from life today. Boys and girls played with toys from infancy until they reached puberty, when they dedicated their playthings to the gods. For children who died before their time, the toys were often placed in their graves.

A child's first toy was frequently a rattle made from brightly painted wood or terra-cotta in the shape of an animal such as a pig with small pellets of clay inside that made a loud noise when shaken. Bells and toy animals of all sorts were also popular, and many have been recovered by archaeologists. When the child was a little older, other toys and activities were available, such as balls, yo-yos, spinning tops, hoops, seesaws, swings, kites, rocking horses, and various games played with knucklebones. Boys were encouraged to play with toy carts and chariots, while girls dressed and cared for well-crafted dolls with movable limbs.

Children often had pets, as seen on Greek vases and relief sculptures. Small dogs were the most popular, but cats, birds, rabbits, mice, and grasshoppers also appear with children in art and literature. Wealthy families such as Sappho's might even afford a monkey imported from Africa. Domestic farm animals were a popular object of entertainment. Anyte, another woman poet, who lived about 300 BC, records what must have been a common scene outside many Greek households:

> *The children put purple reins on you, Mr. Billy Goat,*
> *and a bridle on your bearded throat.*

Athenian grave stele of a young girl with doll and dog
(c. 340 BC).

(HARVARD ART MUSEUMS)

> *They teach you to race your cart around the temple of the*
> *god,*
> *so he may watch them all having their fun.*

Sappho must have also spent time as a child wandering the mountains and glades of Lesbos. Her poems are rich with references to flowers, birds, and the beauties of nature on her island. It's hard not to see a memory of her own childhood in one surviving fragment of her poetry:

> *Evening, you gather together all that shining Dawn has*
> *scattered.*
> *You bring back the sheep, you bring back the goat, you*
> *bring back*
> *the child to its mother.*

EDUCATION IN EARLY Greece was a mixture of both practical and theoretical knowledge. Boys trained their bodies with hunting, riding, and gymnastics and their minds with reading, writing, and arithmetic. Music, dancing, and especially poetry were an essential part of education, with boys memorizing large portions of the songs of Homer. The *Iliad* and the *Odyssey* were, as the ancients believed, the heart of what every boy needed to know about piety, courage, and loyalty. The words of the later Greek rhetorician Heraclitus could just as easily apply to Sappho's day: "From his earliest years, the child beginning his education is given Homer as a nurse for his unformed mind. His poems are swaddling clothes and our minds feed on his milk. He is always there by our side as we grow up."

For a typical Greek girl, however, education would have been much more limited. Learning how to properly manage a household (Greek *oikos*) was central to a young woman's training. The word *oikonomia* or "running of the *oikos*" is, in fact, the root of our word "economics"—the modern economy being seen as a household on a grand scale. But although any female child would have learned all manner of practical skills, it's doubtful she would have gained much beyond basic literacy, if that.

The Greek historian Xenophon wrote a handbook for household management in which he argued that mothers were the primary teachers of girls and instructed them in what they most needed to learn—namely, wool working and self-control. The carding and weaving of wool was essential for making clothing for a family and always fell to the women of the home. A girl who didn't learn this vital skill was unlikely to find a husband. Many of the images of female children in the art of Sappho's time depict girls sitting at the feet of their mothers as they work a loom. There were even wool-working contests in ancient Greece for girls with the greatest skill. Girls in the military-dominated city of Sparta—so often an exception—went far beyond these domestic skills to learn and practice athletic skills just as boys did, but only in preparation for giving birth to stronger sons.

As an aristocratic girl preparing to become a dutiful wife someday, Sappho would have learned all the domestic skills needed, but all we know for certain of Sappho's education is what we can glean from her poetry. She never mentions weaving, aside from garlands of flowers. Instead, what has survived of her work shows a woman thoroughly trained in the Greek literary tradition with a consummate skill in the poetic arts. There are occasional references in later literature to female students in ancient Greek schools—Plato reportedly had two women in his famous Academy, one of whom liked to dress in men's clothing—but there is no solid evidence of such formal institutions during Sappho's day.

It was once fashionable to think of Sappho as the leader of a school for girls like one she herself had presumably been educated in, but there is no evidence for this in her poems. The most reasonable assumption is that either because of coming from an innovative family or because of her own uncompromising effort, Sappho learned the skills needed to perfect herself as a poet. Beyond a doubt, she possessed a remarkable natural talent. Perhaps she joined her brothers as their tutor lectured them in grammar, poetry, and music, or perhaps she was instructed privately by another poet, male or female, who recognized her genius at an early age. All that Sappho's surviving poems tell us is that, as a girl, she learned the rich literary tradition of Greece, especially the poetry of Homer, very well and mastered the difficult techniques of composing various forms of Greek verse.

The musical patterns, or meters, of ancient verse were intricate, complex, and bound by rules that no poet could easily break. Unlike most modern songs, the poetry of the Greeks did not depend on rhyme or accent. What mattered were the number and pattern of long and short syllables within a line.

One common unit was the flowing dactyl (long-short-short, or ♩ ♪ ♪), named for the one long and two short bones of the human finger. The stately spondee (long-long, or ♩♪) was more suitable for solemn songs. There were many possible combinations of patterns, such as Homer's dactylic hexameters, with six dactyls as the basic form. But the most famous type of poetry composed by Sappho (later known as the Sapphic stanza) used shorter lines than Homer's did, with little room for flexibility. To work within the constraints of ancient Greek meter required incredible skill in composition and word choice if a poet aspired to produce the fluid and seemingly effortless verse seen in Sappho.

We can be certain that Sappho also had training during her youth in instrumental music. Sappho is indeed best known for her lyric poetry—that is, poetry composed to be sung to the accompaniment of a lyre. One ancient Greek writer even claimed that Sappho herself invented a popular type of lyre called a *pectis*. A typical lyre was made from a tortoise shell with its hollow side covered by stretched animal skin to form a sound box. Two upright arms of wood or horn were fixed to this shell and joined above by a crossbar on which the strings were fixed over the face of the lyre and secured to a bar at its base. The strings, usually made from gut or sinew, numbered seven or eight and were tuned by being tightened at the crossbar. The strings were plucked with the fingers or with a small stick or quill called a *plectrum*, which Sappho also reportedly invented. Greek vases often show children like young Sappho sitting with a music master and learning the difficult art of playing the lyre.

· · ·

IN HER SURVIVING poems, Sappho gives us only a few hints about the rest of her youth. In one fragment she addresses a girl still too young for marriage:

You seemed to me a small child without grace.

This may reflect Sappho's feelings about herself during the awkward preteen years. In another papyrus fragment she looks back with longing on her girlhood days as she speaks to a friend:

. . . you will remember,
. . . for we in our youth
did these things,
many, beautiful things.

What these beautiful things are Sappho doesn't say, but a rare, firsthand look into the life of girls before the age of marriage comes from another woman poet, Erinna, who lived three centuries after Sappho. In a moving and beautiful poem called *The Distaff,* she laments the death of her childhood friend Baucis and remembers when they were girls:

. . . into a deep wave
you jumped from the white horses with mad running.
"I've got you, my friend," I cried. And when you played
*   the tortoise*
you leapt out and ran through the garden of the courtyard.

*Unhappy Baucis, these are my laments as I weep for you
     deeply,*
*these are your footprints resting still warm in my heart,
     dear girl.*
But what we once loved is now gone.

As young girls we held our dolls in our bedrooms
pretending to be new wives, hearts as yet unbroken.
At dawn your mother handed out wool to the servants,
then came in and called you to help with the salted meat.

*What terror the monster Mormo brought us when we
     were girls.*
*On her head were giant ears and she walked on four
     legs,*
always changing her face.

But when you went to the bed of a man
you forgot all you heard from your mother as a child,
*my dear Baucis. Aphrodite filled your heart with
     forgetfulness.*

We could scarcely hope for a more authentic glimpse of a
girl's life in ancient Greece, and indeed the poem is unique.
Erinna was one of the few female poets aside from Sappho whose
work survives at any length (though barely two pages total in a
book). And although Erinna lived three hundred years later, her
style, language, and emotional content deliberately echo Sappho.

In Erinna's poem she and Baucis play together on the beach—ancient Greek vases show girls skinny-dipping with one another—and then engage in a game of tag called the "tortoise" around the garden. At a sleepover they play dolls and pretend to be new mothers, and then tell ghost stories about a boogeywoman named Mormo to scare each other. Sappho mentions a similar monster, named Gello, who was once a girl herself but died young and then haunted children, snatching them away to death. At last, as dawn breaks, Baucis's mother interrupts their fun and comes to call her daughter to work. As the poem ends, Erinna sings:

> *I weep for you now, absent from your funeral rites,*
> *for my feet may not leave the house and become unclean*
> *nor may I look upon your corpse nor cry with my hair*
> *uncovered.*
> *Blood-red shame makes me weep.*

Whatever ritually polluting circumstance, perhaps childbirth, keeps Erinna away from the last rites of her childhood friend, she mourns deeply for the friend's death and the lost innocence they shared as girls. Next to Sappho, no poet gives us a better window into the interior life of a woman in ancient times.

IN ONE OF her poems, Sappho looks back as an old woman on her girlhood days:

> *my knees that once danced nimbly like fawns cannot carry me*

There were surely many occasions for dancing when Sappho was young, but one sort of occasion must have been the religious festivals and rites that girls throughout Greece celebrated at puberty. This was a crucial transition in a girl's life to mark the time when she set aside childhood things and prepared to take on the task of becoming a wife and mother. It was also a time for the whole community to acknowledge the important role that girls played in religious festivals. For the young women themselves, it was a final chance to form and strengthen bonds of friendship with other girls before the duties and constraints of marriage and children would dominate their lives.

One of the best examples of this sort of religious festival for girls comes from choral songs of the Spartan poet Alcman, who lived in the generation before Sappho. These fragmentary songs were found on papyrus scraps and are known as *partheneia*, or "maiden songs." They were performed at a public all-night festival in Sparta that included dancing and racing. The celebration also served as a kind of coming-out party for the girls, who could show themselves off to potential mates and their families. In the first of Alcman's songs, the girls speak in a single voice in praise of the beauty of their chorus leaders, Hagesichora and Agido. The songs of Alcman are rich in sensual images and homoeroticism, much like the poetry of Sappho:

> *I sing of the light of Agido.*
> *She is like the sun which she calls*

as a witness to shine upon us. Our glorious chorus-leader
does not need me to praise or blame her
in any way, for she shines forth on her own.
She is like a horse set among the grazing herds,
a strong, prize-winning horse with clattering hoofs
as in winged dreams. Do you see her,
like a Venetic race-horse?
But the hair of my cousin Hagesichora gleams
like pure gold.

In another fragment of Alcman, the girls sing of their chorus-leader Astymeloisa as part of a ritual presenting a wreath to Hera, goddess of marriage:

With desire that makes my limbs loose,
she looks upon me more sweetly than sleep or death.
She is not sweet in vain.
Astymeloisa does not answer me,
but holds the wreath
like a star flying through the radiant sky
or like a young golden plant or a soft feather
. . . she moves on slender feet
. . . the moist, delightful perfume Cyprian Cinyras
clings to her virgin hair.

At Athens, there were similar rituals for girls as they grew into women. The Athenian comedy writer Aristophanes includes a key passage in his *Lysistrata*, a brilliant satire about the women of Greece going on a sex strike to force their husbands to stop a destructive war:

> *At seven I became Bearer of Secret Things,*
> *then at ten a Grinder for the goddess.*
> *Later at Brauron I was a Bear in a saffron robe,*
> *finally a lovely young Basket-Bearer wearing a string of*
>   *figs.*

Although the setting of the play is comical, there's little doubt that the sequence of offices here represents a historical reality for at least some girls in ancient Athens. The "Bearers of Secret Things" served at a midsummer night's festival. Two, or perhaps four, of these bearers were chosen from the aristocratic girls of Athens at the age of seven to live in a dwelling on the north slope of the Acropolis. There for a year they dwelled apart, engaged in sacred ceremonies that are not entirely clear, such as weaving a special garment for the goddess Athena and playing a kind of ballgame. On the appointed summer evening, they carried mysterious items into an underground shrine on the Acropolis and returned with something else, also unnamed, wrapped up. Some ancient writers speculated that these were cakes in the form of snakes or phalluses. In any case, it seems the girls were celebrating a fertility festival based on an ancient myth in which the goddess Athena entrusted a baby to the daughters of the first Athenian king, Cecrops, with instructions not to open the basket. The girls couldn't resist the temptation, however, and saw inside the snakelike baby, after which they threw themselves off the Acropolis. The girls who were chosen as Bearers of Secret Things were thus selected to reenact a mysterious ritual central to the community because of their gender, young age, social standing, and purity.

We know little of what the "Grinders" did for the goddess aside from the obvious preparation of presumably sacred grain or what the "Basket-Bearers" carried, but the role of young women serving as "Bears" for Artemis is mentioned elsewhere in ancient literature and represented in Athenian art. Athena was a goddess of the civilized urban life of Athens, but Artemis was a huntress who roamed the woods with her nymphs, and her cult was celebrated in the wild countryside over the mountains on the eastern coast of Athenian territory at Brauron. According to the celebration's origin story, a young girl once teased a bear that in turn attacked her, prompting her brothers to hunt down and slay the animal. Since Artemis was the patron goddess of wild animals, she decreed that she would be appeased only if girls of the city would serve her as bears themselves. Some sources say this role was given only to a select group of girls, but others indicate it was a much wider initiation ritual in which many, if not all, Athenian girls were allowed to participate every few years. Though tantalizingly incomplete, vase paintings of the rituals involved show young women at about the age of puberty running around the sanctuary of the site either nude or wearing saffron-colored skirts.

Since Artemis was a goddess of the transition from girlhood to the adult life of women throughout the ancient Greek world, a celebration similar to this Athenian ritual must have been held for Sappho and her friends on Lesbos. If they were like most Greek girls, they dedicated their toys to the goddess and cut a lock of their hair in symbolic mourning for the end of childhood. The protective goddess Artemis was now left behind as they prepared to enter the new life of active sexuality that was so prominent in the poetry of Sappho—the world of Aphrodite.

2

WEDDING SONGS

Let your bride be four years past puberty and wed her in the fifth.
And be sure to marry a virgin so you can teach her proper ways.

– HESIOD, *WORKS AND DAYS*

THE BYZANTINE *SUDA* encyclopedia says that Sappho was married to a wealthy merchant named Cercylas from the Aegean island of Andros. But there is good reason for believing this is a dirty joke derived from one of the later Greek comedies that unfairly and unflatteringly portray Sappho as sex crazed. Cercylas is an otherwise unknown name deriving from the Greek word for the male reproductive organ (*kerkos*). Andros is a real island lying in the sea between Lesbos and Athens, but its name comes from the Greek word for "male." Therefore, the reference in the *Suda* was likely a laugh line for the comedy audience claiming that Sappho was wed to "Penis from Man Island."

Even though this passage is suspect, it's almost certain that Sappho was married, since the single life was simply not a viable option, especially for a woman, in the ancient Greek world. The social pressures of family and community, as well as the need for children to care for parents in their later years, made marriage a necessity. We also know from Sappho's own poetry that she bore and raised a daughter—a situation that would have been virtually impossible for a woman alone. Regardless of Sappho's sexual preferences, she, like every other Greek woman, was expected to marry and bear children. Perhaps tellingly, she never mentions her husband in her surviving poetry, nor does she write any verses of love in his honor. But whatever his true name and however she felt about him, we can be sure that Sappho had a husband for at least part of her early adult life.

We may know little of Sappho's own married life, but we are fortunate that some of her greatest surviving poetry deals with the subject of marriage itself. Sappho is, in fact, one of our best literary sources on weddings from the early Greek world, and virtually the only window we have into a woman's view of the sudden and sometimes terrifying transition from maiden to wife.

The poet Hesiod, who lived in the decades before Sappho, said that a man should marry when he was about thirty years old. Later Greek writers agree that midthirties was the upper age limit for a man's marriage. This was an ideal; some men married as early as their late teens, but the majority of grooms seemed to have taken a wife at the end of their third decade. This delay was practical, allowing a man to establish himself on his farm or in business so that he could provide for his new family. A man's late thirties was also a time when his father would likely have either retired from active work and handed over the family assets to his son or already have died. If a man did not produce a son until his early thirties and that son waited until *his* thirties to sire his own offspring, there must have been relatively few paternal grandfathers in ancient Greece.

The age for brides was much younger. In Sappho's world, there was no such thing as a prolonged adolescence for girls. Hesiod recommended marriage for women four to five years after puberty, which would have made most brides in their midteens. Girls from wealthy families throughout Greece often married even earlier, many in about their twelfth or thirteenth year. The philosophers Plato and Aristotle encouraged families to wait until a young woman was in her late teens, but this recommendation was probably inspired by the unusual Spartan custom of brides delaying marriage until their eighteenth or even twentieth year.

Greek men would thus have been, on average, fifteen years or more older than their teenage brides. Why would the Greeks practice such a custom? There are several possible answers aside from the need for a man to secure his financial future before marriage. First, a young wife was more easily intimidated and controlled by an older husband. Marriage was not a partnership as much as it was a business transaction in which the wife was often only slightly higher in rank than a sturdy ox. The woman held a crucial but decidedly subordinate role in the marriage relationship. It was her job to bear children and manage the household, not to advise her husband. A typical Greek bride would have little experience in life beyond what was necessary for her to cook, weave, clean, and help as required with the harvest. She would have spent little time outside the home and would have known nothing about the larger world, except what she managed to overhear from her father and brothers. Life for a wealthy girl, such as Sappho, would have offered more opportunities, but in the end a young bride, rich or poor, was a piece of property to be controlled, by harsh measures if necessary.

Another reason for a woman's early marriage was the all-important role of bridal virginity. A man had to know for certain that his wife's sons and thus his heirs were his own. To delay a young woman's age of marriage was to risk the loss of her virginity to another man, in spite of the dreadful consequences such an act would have for her and her family. Under such circumstances, fathers and mothers must have been as eager as any potential husbands for their daughters to marry at an early age. It was also widely believed in the ancient world that a woman's best child-bearing years occurred soon after puberty. Men, by contrast, were thought to have stronger seed when they were older. The fact that many young women died in childbirth because of their physical immaturity seems to have only encouraged the belief that sooner for women was better. If labor and delivery were hard for a teenager, the reasoning went, then it could only grow more difficult as a woman aged.

A final reason why girls were encouraged to marry early was the belief that unmarried girls after puberty were at greater risk for physical and mental instability. A Hippocratic treatise on illnesses affecting virgins states that unmarried young women were prone to disturbing visions and even suicide because the orifice for their menstrual flow had not been properly opened by intercourse with a man. The ancient prescription was simple: frequent sex with a husband and hopefully a resulting pregnancy, which would further aid in achieving balance in both her mind and body.

It's tempting to see the emphasis on bridal virginity simply as a form of masculine oppression against young women, lest they dare to enjoy their own sexuality and thus reduce their value as a commodity for a future husband, but there is more to the story. The evidence we have from Homer, from other archaic Greek poetry, and, most important, from Sappho suggests that women themselves guarded their virginity as a form of empowerment. In Homer's *Odyssey*, the wandering hero Odysseus washes ashore on the island of the Phaeacians and finds there on the beach a beautiful and clever princess named Nausicaa, who is struck by the handsome stranger and sees him as possible husband material. Odysseus tries to win her favor, but Nausicaa is careful to let Odysseus know that, as much as she finds him appealing, she is not about to endanger her reputation, let alone sacrifice her virginity to him there on the shore:

> *I'm afraid of the insolent men in our community who might mock us and of what the worst sort might say if they see us together. . . . They would speak and that would be a scandal against me. I myself would quite disapprove of a girl who acted so.*

Nausicaa insists that Odysseus make his own way to her parents' home and present himself properly before he has any further contact with her.

In a seduction poem by Archilochus, the poet writes a satire against his ex-girlfriend Neoboule, defaming her reputation as a young woman who offered up her most intimate charms to him before marriage. He did this in revenge after her father abruptly broke off his engagement to her. The story that she killed herself in shame is possibly fictional, but the reality of a girl's life being destroyed by even the suggestion of premarital sex with a man was quite real. In the poem, Archilochus delights in seducing another young woman, who seems to be Neoboule's maiden sister, as part of his vengeance against her family:

> *"Don't refuse me dear . . .*
> *Let some other man have Neoboule,*
> *she's over-ripe anyway.*
> *Her virgin bloom has faded away*
> *along with her charm.*
> *She couldn't get enough, you know . . ."*
> *I said such things, and taking the girl*
> *I laid her down, wrapped in a soft cloak,*
> *in the blooming flowers,*
> *my arms embracing her neck.*
> *She was still with fear like a fawn.*
> *I gently took her breasts in my hands,*
> *her fresh skin showed the bloom of youth.*
> *Feeling over her whole body,*
> *I released my vital force,*
> *just touching her golden hair.*

We should perhaps understand that the seducer did not actually penetrate the maiden before he released his "vital force," but her reputation was destroyed in any case. Her bloom, her flower—a common metaphor for virginity in Greek poetry—had now withered in the eyes of any other man, and her value as a wife was ruined. It's hard to imagine a more vicious act of revenge in the ancient Greek world.

The dangers to a young woman's virtue were ever present. In a play by the Athenian poet Aeschylus, a father warns his daughters:

> *I urge you not to slip and fall, my dears.*
> *Remember that you've now attained*
> *the tempting age that turns the heads of men.*
> *A ripe fruit is not easy to protect.*
> *Winged birds and beasts with feet to slither on—*
> *and yes I mean men—ache*
> *to tear it from its branch. How could they not*
> *when Aphrodite has placed such succulence in it*
> *that the juice comes pouring out from beneath the skin?*
> *A maiden's shapely figure is tempting,*
> *the target of every eye, and fingers cannot help*
> *but reach out to pluck it.*

But it's Sappho herself who gives us a woman's thoughts on bridal virginity. In one of her surviving wedding songs, she sings of maidenhood in familiar terms of fruit and flowers, but with a

29

particularly feminine point of view. This poem is pieced together from two separate fragments preserved in different ancient authors, the first from a grammatical commentary by a philosopher named Syrianus who lived at the time the western Roman Empire was collapsing:

> . . . *like the sweet apple that grows red on the lofty branch,*
> *at the very top of the highest bough. The apple-pickers*
>   *have forgotten it*
> *—no, not forgotten, but they could not reach it.*

The second piece is quoted in a manual on literary style by a writer named Demetrius who lived several centuries earlier:

> . . . *like the hyacinth shepherds tread underfoot*
> *in the mountains, and on the ground the purple flower*

These passages may be from a song performed at a wedding banquet or from verses sung at the bridal chamber on the wedding night. The latter could be quite risqué, as we will see, but they could also be sober warnings directed to the unmarried maidens gathered outside the chamber door. Unlike the male voices urging chastity for the sake of family or community values, Sappho makes clear to her female audience that it is in a maiden's own best interest to guard her virginity like an apple out of reach at the topmost branch of a tree. Men will try to pluck it if you let them, but if you value your own body and reputation, you will let them look but not touch.

Sappho doesn't speak of hiding one's fruit away unseen or of withholding the fruit forever; she says simply that it is the woman's responsibility to respect herself and guard her maidenhood until the proper moment. There's no escaping that even in Sappho's poetry, virginity is a commodity to be priced and traded within a patriarchal society, but she warns young women that this is the reality of the world in which they live. A maiden can either throw away her virtue so that it is trampled underfoot like a hyacinth on the mountainside or, like Homer's Nausicaa, take charge of her own body and decide, as much as is within her power, when and to whom she should offer herself.

Sappho makes the irrevocable nature of this decision clear in a poem of two lines, also quoted by Demetrius. With a clever poetic twist, she has a bride after the wedding night address her own departed maidenhood:

> "Virginity, virginity, where have you gone? You've deserted me!"

And her former virginity responds:

> "Never again will I come to you, never again will I come."

For a young woman in ancient Greece, whether she gave herself in youthful passion to a lover in the soft grass of a meadow or to her husband after the marriage ceremony, there was no second chance.

. . .

AN INTRIGUING PASSAGE by the ancient Greek historian Herodotus says the women of Lydia could choose their own husbands. The nearby Asian kingdom of Lydia shows up frequently in the poetry of Sappho and was a major cultural and trading partner with the island of Lesbos. It's at least possible—assuming Herodotus was correct—that the custom of Lydian women having some voice in choosing their spouses made its way across the strait and influenced the way marriages were arranged in Lesbos. Whether this is true or not, some literary and historical evidence suggests that at least in a few cases, a Greek woman could pick her own husband. The sixth-century-BC aristocrat Callias reportedly granted his daughters the unusual gift of choosing their own spouses from the entire eligible male population of Athens. It was also said that Helen of Troy was allowed by her father, Tyndareus, to select her mate. And of course Odysseus's wife, Penelope, organizes the famous contest of the bow in Homer's *Odyssey* to see which man will take her husband's place:

> *Come now, you suitors, here is your prize set before you.*
> *Your challenge is*
> *to take the bow of godlike Odysseus, and whoever will*
> *most easily string it and*
> *shoot an arrow through all twelve axes, with him I will*
> *go.*

But these few instances of a Greek wife choosing her own husband are either of questionable historical validity or in the realm of myth. For most, if not all, Greek women in real life, the decision about who she would marry lay with her father or the male relative who held legal guardianship over her. If her father was dead, her guardian probably would have been her eldest brother or an uncle. But whoever the man was who chose her husband, the decision must have been anything but simple. A loving father, as most Greek men surely were, would not have wanted to make a match for his daughter that left her unhappy or open to physical or psychological abuse by someone who was often a much older man she barely knew. And we can be sure that the mother who had invested so much time in raising a girl would make her opinion clear to her husband in private. For a poor girl, the options would have been limited. For a young woman of the wealthy nobility like Sappho, the possibilities were much greater, stretching even beyond the shores of her island. The idea that she married "Penis from Man Island" is certainly fiction, but the suggestion that her husband was a wealthy merchant is quite plausible, given the trading and business connections of Sappho's family.

What qualities would a Greek husband look for in a potential mate? In many ways, Odysseus's faithful Penelope was the ideal. She was unwaveringly loyal to her long-absent husband, a devoted mother to their son, Telemachus, a hardworking manager of her family's household, and intelligent and innovative while still being submissive to her spouse. The ghost of Agamemnon—

murdered by his own, faithless wife, Clytemnestra—praises Penelope when he speaks from Hades:

> *O fortunate son of Laertes, Odysseus of many twists and*
> * turns,*
> *surely you have won yourself a wife of great virtue.*
> *The heart of blameless Penelope, daughter of Icarius, was*
> * proven good.*
> *How well she has remembered you, her wedded husband.*
> * The fame of her*
> *virtue will never die, but the gods will make for the*
> * people of earth a thing of*
> *grace in the song for prudent Penelope.*

But such women were rare in the minds of Greek men. Hesiod sings of the creation of the beautiful Pandora, the first of all women, as a curse by Zeus and warns his male audience:

> *A man couldn't gain anything better than a good wife,*
> *just as nothing could be worse than a bad one*
> *—a freeloader who roasts her husband without a fire*
> *and serves him up raw old age.*

The Greek poet Semonides, who lived on the Aegean island of Amorgós, in the generation before Sappho, provides grooms with a primer on the different types of women they might choose from. The misogyny of the poem is meant to be humorous, but, like Hesiod's unfavorable descriptions of women, it must

have expressed the underlying prejudice of many Greek men in
Sappho's age:

In the beginning Zeus created many kinds of women
with various minds.
He made one from a hairy sow.
Her house is filthy with mud and all those inside it are
disheveled and roll in the dirt. This pig-woman sits
    around unwashed
in dirty clothes among the dunghills and grows fat . . .
The god made another woman from the mischievous fox.
Her mind gets into everything. No act of wickedness is
    unknown to her,
no act of good either . . .
Another was created from a donkey, dusty grey and
    stubborn.
It's devilishly difficult to get her to work. You have to curse
    and tug
to get her going . . .
Another the god made from a maned, prim mare.
She avoids all housework and the chores of slaves.
She wouldn't dream of touching the grain mill or of lifting
    a sieve
or sweeping the dung out of doors . . .
But Zeus also made a woman from the bee.
It's a lucky man who gets her, blameless as she is.
A man's life grows and blossoms under her touch.
She loves her husband and he loves her in return.

They grow old together and their glorious children rise to fame.

In spite of such generally negative views of women in early Greek poetry, we shouldn't assume that marriage was a loveless institution tolerated by men (and women) merely for the sake of producing children and providing security in old age. Most husbands and wives, even though they may have been strangers at their wedding, must have taken their vows full of hope that love would grow between them as time passed. Some of the most beautiful expressions of married love in all of literature come from the poet Homer writing in the century before Sappho. When the Trojan hero Hector hurriedly speaks to his wife, Andromache, on the walls of the besieged city before a great battle, she urges him to stay:

> *For me it would be better to go down to the grave than*
> *   lose you,*
> *for never more will peace be mine when you have met*
> *   your fate,*
> *only woes. Neither father nor queenly mother do I have . . .*
> *Hector, you are to me as a father and royal mother, you are*
> *   like my brother,*
> *and you are my own vigorous husband.*

And when the divine Calypso offers the wandering Odysseus eternal life if he will stay with her on her island of paradise, he refuses her so that he might see his beloved wife again:

Mighty goddess, do not be angry with me. I know very
    well that wise
Penelope is less beautiful than you to look upon, for she is
    only mortal while you
are immortal and ageless. But even so, I yearn endlessly to
    reach my home
again and see the day of my return.

Such expressions of love are poetic ideals, but if Homer truly embodied the best that a man might aspire to in life, the desire for true love with a woman in marriage could be as real as his hope for honor and glory.

THE FORMAL MARRIAGE between a man and a woman in ancient Greece began with a betrothal ceremony, similar to a modern engagement. The details varied by time and place, but at its core it was a contract between the bride's father or guardian and her future husband. Witnesses were in attendance, though the bride, if she was present at all, played no role in the ceremony. The fourth-century-BC Athenian writer Menander probably portrays the brief ritual accurately in a play found on a piece of papyrus in Egypt:

FATHER: *I give you this girl so that she may bring children*
    into this world within the bounds of marriage.
GROOM: *I accept her.*
FATHER: *I agree to give you a dowry of three talents for her.*
GROOM: *I accept that too, with pleasure.*

The marriage ceremony may have taken place soon after, or if the girl was still too young, there may have been a gap of several years between the betrothal and the wedding. The dowry was a payment by the bride's father to seal the contract. If the groom repudiated his betrothed before or after the wedding, the money or goods would have to be returned to the bride's family. This consequence provided an important incentive for a husband to honor his commitments. In Homeric times, which may more accurately reflect the customs of Sappho's Lesbos, the groom reciprocated by making gifts to the bride's family when a marriage was pledged.

As for the marriage ceremony itself, we can use the poetry of Sappho to piece together what wedding festivities in Lesbos must have been like, at least for the wealthy nobility. The celebration centered on the *ekdosis*, literally the "giving away" of the bride to the bridegroom, beginning with the physical transfer of the bride from the house of her father to that of her new husband. If the bride was a foreign woman, a procession from the ship in port to the new home was in order.

One of Sappho's most complete songs surviving on papyrus takes this very theme as its subject. It celebrates the return of the Trojan prince Hector as he brings home his bride, Andromache, but the scene is not found in Homer. What we have instead is a joyous celebration outside the epic tradition that, in all likelihood, represents the marriage procession of an aristocratic man and woman in ancient Lesbos. Sappho may have composed the song for performance at a particular wedding, perhaps one in which a foreign bride was brought to the island, but it could just as easily be that the poem was used to celebrate the arrival of any bride at her new home. By looking closely at the verses, we can learn some important details about Sappho's world and reconstruct at least a partial picture of what the festivities of a wedding in her own time must have been like:

> *Cyprus . . .*
> *the herald came . . .*
> *Idaeus, the swift messenger . . .*
> *". . . and the rest of Asia . . . undying glory.*
> *Hector and his companions are bringing the lively-eyed,*
> *graceful Andromache from holy Thebe and ever-flowing*
> *Placia in their ships over the salty sea, along with many*
>> *golden bracelets*
> *and perfumed purple robes, beautifully-painted ornaments*
> *and countless silver cups and ivory."*
> *So he spoke. Quickly Hector's dear father rose up*
> *and the news spread among his friends in the spacious*
>> *city.*
> *At once the sons of Ilus yoked mules to the*
> *smooth-running carts, then the whole crowd*
> *of women and maidens with . . . ankles climbed on board.*
> *The daughters of Priam apart . . .*
> *the young men yoked horses to chariots . . .*
> *in great style . . .*
> *charioteers . . .*
> *. . . like the gods*

. . . holy together
set out . . . to Ilium
the sweet-sounding flute and the cithara mingled
and the sound of castanets. Maidens sang a holy song
and a wondrous echo reached to the sky . . .
everywhere in the streets was . . . mixing-bowls and
    drinking cups . . .
myrrh and cassia and frankincense mingled.
The older women cried out with joy
and all the men erupted in a high-pitched shout
calling on Paean, far-shooting god skilled with the lyre.
They sang in praise of god-like Hector and Andromache.

One of the most striking features of this poem is that Sappho composed it using a type of Homeric meter rather than the shorter lines she normally favored. Even the particular Greek words and phrasing are a deliberate echo of Homer rather than the dialect of Sappho's native Lesbos. Yet the result is not a poor imitation of epic, but a transformation of the genre into something entirely different. The meter so often used for bloody battles becomes the instrument of an exultant celebration of a new life for a man and woman. If Sappho sang this song at a wedding feast, it must have been striking to watch her rise with her lyre and begin the formal rhythm of epic, but to sing instead of the love and laughter and joy of a marriage. It is a masterful achievement of a poet who is so skilled in a traditional style of poetry that she can transform it into something entirely different.

Athenian pyxis showing a wedding procession with the bride
driven in a chariot from her parents' home to that of her husband
(fifth century BC).

(BRITISH MUSEUM)

The poem begins with a broken fragment containing a single
word, "Cyprus," followed by a break in which several words have
been lost. Cyprus was the island home of Aphrodite, goddess
of love and sex, so the song's opening is probably an invocation

of a deity of fertility most appropriate for the joining of a man and woman in marriage. The chief Trojan herald, a breathless Idaeus known from the *Iliad*, then arrives at the palace of Priam to announce to the king in suitably Homeric fashion that his son Hector has returned from his short voyage to the south with his bride, the lively-eyed and graceful Andromache, daughter of King Eëtion of Thebe. With her are many bridal gifts from her father, including golden bracelets, perfumed purple robes, painted ornaments, silver cups, and ivory. The wealth of these gifts points to a vast trade network of early Greece, and Sappho's Lesbos in particular. Purple dye, for example, came from a shellfish found on the Lebanese coast, while ivory (Greek *elephas*) was an expensive luxury item carved from the tusks of Asiatic or African elephants.

The herald's announcement rouses the whole palace, indeed the whole city, into action. The young men, descendants of Ilus, founder of Ilium (Troy), yoke mules to the carts for the women and maidens. In Sappho's Lesbos, the women are as much a part of the public celebration as the men. Stylish chariots are readied for the daughters of Priam, and the charioteers drive them to the harbor to welcome their brother and his bride.

After an unknown number of missing lines, we find ourselves in the middle of a musical celebration as Hector drives Andromache into the city surrounded by jubilant well-wishers on all sides. The bride's procession in a chariot to her new home is, in fact, a favorite theme on vases found throughout the Greek world. Flutes, cithara harps, and castanets, along with maidens singing wedding songs, welcome the happy couple into

Troy. Bowls of wine are mixed and shared, while the burning of imported incense marks the religious importance of the festivities. This poem of Sappho is the earliest reference to incense in Greek literature. Frankincense and myrrh are not found in Homer, suggesting that these aromatic resins imported from southern Arabia had just arrived in the Greek world in Sappho's day, though they had long been known in Egypt.

The climax of the song is a chorus of the whole city. Old women cry out in joy, and men join in with a ritual song addressed to Paean, the god Apollo. In the final line, Hector and Andromache are significantly described as godlike (*theoeikeloi*), a deliberately Homeric word often used for heroes in battle, but here transformed into an epithet for a groom and his bride. As with the rest of the poem, the conclusion is a striking use of epic language by Sappho transformed for her own purposes.

In most marriages in Lesbos and throughout ancient Greece, this procession of the bride to her new home probably occurred later in the wedding day, after feasting and songs at the home of the young woman's father. We're again fortunate that Sappho preserves different stages of the wedding festivities in her poems, though it's not always clear which songs belong to which part of the celebration.

One such fragmentary and enigmatic Sapphic poem is considerably shorter than the previous song of Hector and Andromache:

> . . . *for once you were a child*
> . . . *come sing these things*

. . . talk to us, grant us
your favors.

For we are going to a wedding, as you
well know. But as quickly as possible,
send away the virgins.
May the gods have . . .

. . . a road to great Olympus
. . . for mortals

If this is a choral wedding song, as seems likely, the setting appears to be a group of young women en route to a marriage celebration. They come upon an older woman along the way and ask her to share her memories and wisdom of such events in her own life. The driving off of the maidens may be an encouragement to them to find husbands of their own as soon as possible, or it could be part of the ritual separation of the bride from her childhood companions before she begins the next stage of her life with the wedding night.

The last, broken lines are particularly puzzling. Is the joy of marriage optimistically compared to a trip to heavenly Olympus, or does the missing space in the papyrus before the line warn more darkly that "(there is not) a road to great Olympus for mortals," so we better grab what joy from life we can? The latter is a thought expressed by the Spartan poet Alcman. "No mortal may go soaring to the heavens," he declares—a thought more in keeping with the pessimism of the ancient Greeks. Since Sappho strikes most readers as a romantic yet realistic poet, we may well assume that her final lines reflect the latter mood.

Another song of Sappho, preserved in Hephaestion's second-century-AD book on poetic meter, may also have been performed at weddings. It's a remarkable little poem in that it expresses feminine sexuality in a way not found in male Greek writers:

> *Truly, sweet mother, I cannot weave on the loom,*
> *for I am overcome with desire for a boy because of slender*
> *Aphrodite.*

What is so compelling about these deceptively simple lines is that the young woman is allowed to express her desire in such an open way. While sitting with her mother in the familiar environment of her home working the loom as all good Greek girls did, in a moment of exasperation she confesses that she is overwhelmed not with *eros* ("love, passion") but an even more powerful emotion, *pothos*—the same word used of Alexander the Great to describe his desire to conquer the world. Proper Greek maidens as found in male authors did not express such emotions, their sexuality being rarely if ever acknowledged. Only in a female writer like Sappho could a young woman find the safe space to express these feelings.

The word Sappho uses for the object of the girl's affection is also telling. Greek *pais* (translated "boy" here) is usually reserved for a child or young person of either gender, meaning the girl is presumably in love with a young man—or conceivably a young woman—of her own age, not an older groom. If this poem was performed publicly at a wedding, it shows an amazing openness to youthful female sexuality in ancient Lesbos. Of course, it may never have been intended to be a wedding song, but rather a private poem composed by Sappho for her friends. The subject matter may have been simply too shocking for a male audience to hear.

Other songs of Sappho strike a more conventional chord of praising both the bride and the groom at a wedding, but in ways that may sometimes surprise a modern audience. In a papyrus fragment dating to the late second or early third century AD, Sappho praises a:

> . . . bride with beautiful feet

This may seem like an odd compliment, but in the earlier Greek poetic tradition, Homer portrays the goddess Hera as having "shining feet," and Hesiod praises a divine daughter of Ocean with "beautiful ankles." To describe a mortal bride as having lovely feet is therefore to liken her to a goddess. There is also an element of class to the praise, since delicate feet were a sign of the leisure enjoyed by aristocratic women, unlike those who spent their lives toiling on a farm.

Another passage from Hephaestion's metrical handbook records one of Sappho's wedding songs addressed to both the groom and bride:

> Blessed bridegroom, your wedding has been accomplished
> just as you prayed and you have the maiden bride you
> desired.

Your form is graceful and your eyes . . .
honey-sweet. Love pours over your lovely face . . .
. . . Aphrodite has greatly honored you

The first stanza is addressed to the groom, but the second addresses the bride. Here the word for "love" pouring over the young woman's face like honey is the more conventional *eros*, with the implication of desire for her new husband within the proper context of marriage.

Other lines of Sappho quoted by the literary critic Dionysius in the first century BC, which he describes as from a wedding song of Sappho, tell the groom to appreciate what he has been given:

for never,
bridegroom, was there another girl like this one.

And Sappho offers this final wedding praise for the groom, again from Hephaestion:

To what, dear bridegroom, can I in handsomeness
 compare you?
To a slender sapling most of all I do compare you.

The Greek word for "sapling" here (*orpex*) is often used for off-spring as well. As a firm and flexing rod, the implied comparison to the groom's genitals would not escape the revelers at the wedding feast.

At the conclusion of the marriage feast, the bride was escorted by the groom to her new home while well-wishers followed behind:

Farewell, bride, farewell, much-honored bridegroom

sings Sappho in two similar fragments. At the groom's home, the couple was escorted to the wedding chamber where the marriage would be consummated and the young woman would make the physical transition from maiden to wife. Here the groom would "loosen the pure virgin's girdle," as Sappho's contemporary Alcaeus puts it in his poem on the wedding of the mortal Peleus and the goddess Thetis, parents of the hero Achilles.

As if the moment weren't terrifying enough for the young woman, it was traditional for guests who had followed the couple to their new home to gather outside the bedchamber and sing risqué songs called *epithalamia* while the pair made love for the first time. This lewd and ribald charivari probably has its origin in ancient fertility rituals meant to encourage pregnancy and deflect the attention of any jealous gods away from the amorous actions of the couple. It must have also been great fun for the wedding guests, who likely would have been quite intoxicated by this point. To keep unwanted intruders from the chamber so that the couple might carry out the business at hand, a sturdy doorkeeper was appointed to guard the bedroom. It seems, too, that a symbolic attempt by the bride's friends to rescue her from her new husband was part of the festivities.

The prudish grammarian Demetrius apparently didn't approve of such activities, writing, "Sappho makes cheap fun of the rustic bridegroom and the door-keeper at the wedding, using vulgar rather than poetic language." More than fifteen hundred years after Sappho, a Byzantine churchman was still complaining about her vulgar wedding songs. But Demetrius and others failed to appreciate that a gifted poet can compose equally great works both sublime and profane, depending on the occasion. The entrance of the bridegroom into the wedding chamber is, in fact, celebrated in one of Sappho's most famous and thoroughly bawdy songs:

> *Raise high the roof—*
> *Hymenaeus!*
> *Raise it up, carpenters—*
> *Hymenaeus!*
> *The bridegroom is coming, the equal of Ares,*
> *and he's much bigger than a big man.*

Or, as J. D. Salinger puts it in the title of his novella borrowed from this poem, *Raise High the Roof Beam, Carpenters.* What allegedly makes the raising of the roof necessary is the giant erection of the approaching bridegroom in anticipation of bedding his bride. His penis is so large that he is compared to enormous Ares, the god of war, who is a frequent symbol of unrestrained masculinity. The traditionally invoked Hymenaeus was a god of marriage whose name derives from the soon-to-be-ruptured hymen of the bride.

The doorkeeper is also the brunt of phallic humor in Sappho. The relationship between the size of a man's feet and his penis is an ancient one:

> *The door-keeper's feet are as long as seven outstretched*
> > *arms,*
> *and his sandals are made from five ox-hides,*
> *ten cobblers labored hard to make them.*

The revelry outside the chamber apparently could go on through the night. In a final fragmentary papyrus, Sappho sings of maidens gathered outside the bedroom until the dawn, calling to the groom:

> *virgins . . .*
> *all night long . . .*
> *might sing of the love between you and the bride*
> > *with violets in her lap.*

> *But rise up! Call the young men*
> *your own age, so that we may see*
> *less sleep than the . . .*
> > *with a clear voice.*

But now that the marriage has been properly consummated, the sensual *eros* of the wedding celebrations has been replaced by another Greek word for love, *philotes*, a more subdued and proper term to honor the relations between a husband and wife.

.   .   .

NONE OF SAPPHO'S surviving poetry mentions the duties of a wife, but we can use other ancient sources to create a picture of what was expected from a woman after marriage. In classical Athens, wives led a very restricted life hidden from the gaze of men outside their family, but in the age of Sappho there seems to have been more latitude for married women to move freely about in society, though always within the boundaries set for them by men.

The poems of Homer provide some of the best hints about the daily life of aristocratic women in early Greece. Epic poetry is not history, but the values shown in the *Iliad* and *Odyssey* are as close as we are likely to get to those shared by the upper-class men and women of Sappho's Lesbos. The ideal wife in Homer is, as we've seen already, Penelope, faithful spouse of Odysseus, while the paradigm of the troublesome woman is Helen of Troy.

As the *Odyssey* opens, Odysseus has been gone from his island home of Ithaca for almost twenty years fighting at Troy and then wandering the world. Greedy suitors press Penelope to remarry so that they can control the kingdom and wealth of her husband. But she has a son who has almost reached the age when he can inherit his father's property, so she is determined to preserve his inheritance for him. The household is threatened by disloyal servants, and Odysseus's father, Laertes, has withdrawn to the country in despair. The future of Penelope's family has fallen on her shoulders—and she rises to the occasion.

Odysseus may be fighting monsters and journeying to the

land of the dead, but the odyssey of Penelope is just as perilous. Yet in the midst of these enormous threats, the wife of Odysseus continues to hope and prepare for his return. She manages the household, raises their son, weaves clothing, and never shares her bed with another man. Helen, on the other hand, abandons her husband, Menelaus, to run off to Troy with a handsome young prince named Paris. On the walls of Troy she calls herself a whore, though there seems to be little regret in her voice. Even when the Greeks win the war and she returns with Menelaus to Sparta, the tension between the two is thick enough to cut with a knife.

When Odysseus's son, Telemachus, comes to visit in search of his father, Helen assures him she was secretly on the side of the Greeks:

> *The rest of the Trojan women cried in grief, but not me.*
> *My heart, which had changed by now, leapt up and I*
> *yearned*
> *to sail back home again. I grieved too late for the madness*
> *sent by Aphrodite, luring me to Troy, far from my dear*
> *land,*
> *abandoning my own child, my bridal bed, my husband too,*
> *a man lacking in neither brains nor handsome form.*

Menelaus then responds with dripping sarcasm: "*That* was a tale, my dear—so well told." He continues, telling Telemachus how Odysseus saved them when Helen tried to betray the Greeks as they hid inside the wooden horse at Troy:

You came along, Helen—roused no doubt by some dark
    power bent on
giving glory to Troy—accompanied by your dashing
    young Prince Deiphobus.
Three times you walked around the hollow horse, feeling
    and stroking its flanks,
challenged our warriors, calling them by name.

Yours was the voice of their long-absent wives.

Theirs is not a happy marriage. Helen is every bit as intelligent and capable as Penelope, but she uses her beauty and her wits to weaken rather than strengthen her husband and his honor.

In his poetry, Homer does offer one hint about the particular qualities of the women of Lesbos themselves. When Agamemnon is trying to appease Achilles so that he will return to the war and fight again for the Greeks, he offers Achilles seven female slaves from Lesbos, making a point that they are both beautiful and highly skilled at household work. These are not wives, but servants, though the attributes valued by men in both were similar.

In the centuries after Homer and Sappho, the expectations put on Greek wives changed little, though their freedoms seem to have become more restricted. One of the clearest pictures we have of these expectations comes from the early-second-century-AD writer Plutarch, who composed a handbook for brides called *Advice on Marriage*. In it he urges husbands to be patient and understanding of their spouses, but he expects wives to make any necessary adjustments to married life. He begins by urging women to remember that the Athenian wise man Solon, who lived at the same time as Sappho, urged wives to eat the sweet fruit of a quince before getting into bed with their husbands so that their speech might be delightful.

This is followed by more practical advice from Plutarch himself, such as:

- A good wife ought to be visible only when she is with her husband. When he is not present, she should hide herself away.

- The harmony between a man and a woman should be like music, but it is he who leads and makes the decisions.

- A married woman ought not to shrink away when her husband wants to make love but embrace him with appropriate enthusiasm. On the other hand, she should never initiate sex. This is the behavior of a prostitute, not a wife.

- A wife should not make friends on her own, but restrict herself to those who are known to and approved of by her husband.

- A wife should realize she is never going to get along with her mother-in-law. Still, she should try her best to be friendly with her.

If a husband found his wife displeasing in bed, there were other socially acceptable options available to him. As one ancient writer put it: "We have prostitutes for sexual pleasure, mistresses to look after our daily comforts, and wives for the procreation of legitimate children and to act as managers of our households." Or, as the Greek historian Xenophon said: "Surely you don't think men have children with their wives because of sexual desire, when the streets and brothels are full of women who can satisfy such needs?"

Slave women of his own household were natural and convenient targets of a man's desires, but for a modest fee, a man could engage the company of a professional prostitute—or for a few coins more, an evening with one of the high-class *hetairai*, the companions often pictured on ancient Greek drinking cups. These latter women were idealized as petite and graceful, with small, firm breasts and great dexterity. Unlike common prostitutes, they were skilled not only in giving sexual pleasure, but also in music and conversation. As they aged and began to lose their physical appeal, they were forced to engage in much more coarse sexual acts (also pictured vividly on cups) that no *hetaira* in her prime and certainly no proper wife would ever consider. The only limit on men's sexual liaisons recognized by law was adultery with a married woman, which was seen as the abuse of another man's property and was reportedly punishable in ancient Athens by the offending man's having a large radish or mullet fish rammed into his anus.

Wives may not have liked it when their husbands sought companionship elsewhere, but they were expected to bear it with grace and not complain. Needless to say, no such options for sexual adventures, at least with men, were allowed to married women. A woman who committed adultery faced immediate divorce, as a mark of shame was forbidden to wear jewelry, and was banned from participation in the all-important public religious ceremonies.

But a wife need not be unfaithful to her husband to face the trauma of divorce. A man could dissolve a marriage simply by expelling his wife from their home. A wife seeking the end of a marriage on the other hand, faced much greater difficulties. She would need to seek the approval and help of her father or former guardian. Even if her wish was granted, the prospects of returning in shame to her parents' house and the unlikelihood that another man would marry her and provide the economic security a woman needed must have discouraged all but the bravest or wealthiest women from pursuing such action. In the minds of most women, a bad husband must have seemed preferable to separation from her children, as it was their father who retained custody of any sons and daughters she produced. For in the ancient Greek world of Sappho, children were the center of a woman's life.

3

A MOTHER'S LOVE

I have a beautiful child who is like golden flowers
in form, my beloved Cleis, for whom
I would not take all of Lydia . . .

– SAPPHO, POEM 132

FOR SAPPHO SCHOLARS, one of the most exciting discoveries from Oxyrhynchus was a fragmentary papyrus scroll written in the early centuries AD that contains a short biography of the poet no more than a paragraph long. The entry on Sappho includes a line written in Greek that says "she had a daughter named Cleis named after her own mother." This fragment is centuries older than the Byzantine *Suda* encyclopedia that also mentions Cleis. Sappho's father, mother, and three brothers are listed, but the papyrus doesn't name the father of Cleis. This is a surprising omission in a world where a child's identity was so closely connected with his or her father. Perhaps the author of the papyrus knew about the tradition that Sappho was married to Cercylas ("Penis from Man Island") but rejected it as absurd. Or perhaps the writer simply didn't know who the father was.

In any case, the importance of the papyrus is that eight hundred years after Sappho lived, it affirms the tradition that she had a daughter named Cleis, whom she herself celebrates in her songs.

The first and longest of Sappho's poems to mention Cleis comes from the oldest surviving fragments of her songs. It is the same poem, mentioned in Chapter 1, that contains the sole reference to Sappho's mother:

For my mother used to say
that when she was young it was
a great ornament if someone had her hair
bound in a purple headband.

But for a girl whose hair
is yellower than
a flaming torch . . .

crowns adorned with
blooming flowers.
Recently a decorated headband

. . . from Sardis
. . . cities

But for you, Cleis, I have no beautiful headband
nor do I know how to get one.
But the one in Mytiline . . .

. . . to have

. . . adorned

. . . these things of the family of Cleanax

. . . exile

. . . memories dreadfully wasted away

This badly damaged poem is pieced together from two papyrus fragments, one residing in Copenhagen and the other in Milan, that were revealed to the public just as the Second World War was beginning. Exactly where they originated is unknown, but the style and writing of the scribes place them in Egypt in the third century BC—over five hundred years earlier than most papyri from the garbage dump at Oxyrhynchus. This is still a gap of four hundred years from the lifetime of the poet herself, but these precious bits of writing may be the oldest record we will ever have of Sappho's poetry.

The context of the poem is uncertain, but the tone is one of longing and regret, with Sappho apologizing to her daughter. She has no way to give Cleis a beautiful and expensive headband from Sardis in Lydia, such as she must have worn herself when she was a girl. Such a decorated purple headband would be available in Mytilene, the chief city of Lesbos, but they are not living there. The rival clan of the Cleanactidae, the family of Cleanax, is now in power and has apparently driven out Sappho's family. Sappho may be somewhere else on the island, but a more reasonable guess is that this song was composed when she was in exile in Sicily. Her daughter Cleis has accompanied her there and is old enough to wish for the finer things in life that she sees the girls around her wearing. It breaks Sappho's heart that she is unable to give her child what she had in her youth. She describes the hair of Cleis as "yellower than a flaming torch," using a term (*xanthe*) for golden often mixed with shades of red, the same Greek word used by Homer for the fair hair of the heroes Achilles and Odysseus. If Cleis looked like her mother, perhaps Sappho also had golden hair.

The second fragment in which Sappho mentions her daughter is quoted by the second-century-AD scholar Hephaestion in his book on poetic meters. This short piece expresses Sappho's love for her child in a most moving way that any mother would understand:

> *I have a beautiful child who is like golden flowers*
> *in form, my beloved Cleis, for whom*
> *I would not take all of Lydia or lovely . . .*

The word here for "golden" (*chrusios*) is different from the term used for Cleis's hair in the previous verses, but the effect of a radiant, shining girl is much the same, with the metaphor extended to her whole form (*morpha*), not just her hair. She is like golden flowers, or more specifically, like a bloom of flowers from head to toe. The word translated as "beloved" is *agapata*, an adjective form of the noun *agape* later used by Christians to express the love of God for the world. Sappho didn't invent the term, but she is among the first to use it, with Homer reserving it only for sons.

Sappho closes the fragment with the declaration that she would not trade her child for "all of Lydia"—the epitome of riches and luxury in her day—"or lovely . . . ," but there the poem breaks off. The second thing she wouldn't trade Cleis for is absent, but some scholars have guessed that the missing word is "Lesbos," perhaps indicating that this poem, too, was composed in exile.

The last of Sappho's songs that may refer to Cleis barely deserves to be called a poem, since it is in such a woefully fragmentary state. It comes from a scrap of papyrus found at Oxyrhynchus and now preserved at Oxford University. The text is from a commentary on lyric poetry from the first or second century AD by an unknown author, who says:

> About Cleis later on she says this also:
> "but if me . . . you looked at . . . the gods give wealth . . ."

One of several problems with this brief fragment is that the name Cleis isn't actually present on the papyrus, only a final letter that may be from her name. Most of the other words have letters missing as well, so we would be foolish to place too much faith in this broken poem. But if the verse is indeed about Cleis, we might not be amiss in reading the line as a touching phrase by Sappho comparing the look of Cleis to a gift from the gods.

As we have said, arguing on the grounds of what Sappho doesn't say in her surviving poems is problematic. But the fact that she mentions only one daughter and that ancient commentators who had access to all her songs refer to a single child suggests, at least tentatively, that Cleis was Sappho's sole offspring.

If this is true, it was an unusual situation for a woman in Sappho's time and may suggest one reason why her love for Cleis was so strong.

In ancient Greece, women prided themselves on the number of children, especially sons, that they bore and raised. For a woman to have a single child—and a girl at that—would have earned her scarcely less pity than if she were barren. A mother with no sons would have no heirs for her husband and no man to care for her as she grew older. It's certainly possible that Sappho had other children and that she chose not to mention them in her poems or that such poems didn't survive, but all we can be sure of is that she had a daughter. If we dare to speculate even further, Cleis seems to have been all the more precious to Sappho because she was her only child. Perhaps for this reason, Sappho does something quite unusual for an ancient Greek writer by celebrating her daughter, her own beloved Cleis, in some of her most beautiful poetry.

MALE AUTHORS FROM classical times rarely discuss pregnancy and birth. It's likely that most found the process mysterious and distasteful. The few references we do have are most commonly from medical texts by men who were often mistaken about the basics of female anatomy and physiology. But enough survives on subjects such as fertility, conception, pregnancy, and childbirth that we can create a picture of how these subjects were viewed, at least by men, in the ancient world. The results are often amusing and sometimes frightful.

A woman's primary role in ancient Greece was to produce children. However, no one—at least among men—was quite sure how this happened, aside from being the obvious result of sexual intercourse. Male doctors discussed and wrote about various theories of fertility and pregnancy, but we have no surviving records from female practitioners, though we know they existed. Men in the medical profession seemed, in fact, to take great offense at the notion that women might have some insight into reproduction that they did not. Theory usually took precedence over empirical observation, while anatomical knowledge was hampered by the fact that dissection of human bodies was forbidden on religious grounds. The writings of doctors reveal that they could not agree on how or where a man's seed was formed, what conditions were best for pregnancy, or whether a woman contributed anything to the process of conception.

The prevailing view among ancient doctors and men in general was that women were simply incubators for men. As the playwright Aeschylus says at the conclusion of his *Oresteia* trilogy:

> *The mother is not the begetter of the child, merely the nurse of the newly-implanted seed.*

Authorities such as Aristotle heartily agreed, but a few medical writers conceded that a mother might have some role in determining the sex and characteristics of her child. It was also thought that the mental state of a woman at the moment of conception could be influential. One ancient medical text tells the story of a notably ugly man from Cyprus who reportedly had his wife look at beautiful statues while they had sex so that she would bear shapely children.

Virtually all Greek medical writers agreed that conception was a tricky and delicate business. It was supposed that the mouth of the womb had to close immediately after intercourse so that the woman would retain the man's seed. Aristotle also advised that the uterus should be anointed with cedar oil, lead ointment, or frankincense mixed with olive oil to help the sperm stay in place as long as possible. Insertion into the vagina of a clump of wool dipped in ox marrow or the burning of incense made from sulfur, garlic, and beaver testicles was thought to be helpful. Other aids to conception included a woman having a meal and a massage before intercourse and abstaining from wine. Sex during the waxing moon was also advised, on the grounds that actions in the heavens influenced fertility here on earth. It was also believed that men with exceptionally long penises were less fertile because their sperm would cool down too much by the time it was deposited in the vagina.

A woman's role as a producer of children was taken as seriously by wives as by husbands, and the failure to produce a child could be devastating for a young bride. Archaeologists have uncovered numerous inscriptions by women making pilgrimages to sacred sites, such as the temple of the healing god Asclepius at Epidaurus in southern Greece, to pray for a child. Some women left behind small clay models of their wombs as offerings for a successful pregnancy. Women who were not able to become pregnant were often seen as cursed by the gods and subject to divorce on grounds of barrenness. Men, aside from the well-endowed already noted, seldom bore any responsibility for infertility.

Medical knowledge about fertility increased slowly over the centuries from Sappho's time to the end of the classical world. It was left to the Roman-era writer Plutarch to offer the most enlightened and balanced view of conception from ancient times: "Nature . . . takes a portion from each partner and mixes it together, producing offspring that are common to both, so that neither the man or woman can distinguish what is his or hers."

ALTHOUGH A WOMAN'S chief concern was producing children, there were occasions when she would want to prevent pregnancy. These included having several healthy children already, a shortage of food, or concerns about her own health if she bore another child. Contraception doesn't feature largely in ancient medical texts, because of the emphasis on fertility and the availability of infant exposure as an after-the-fact birth control method, but also because most doctors seemed to have viewed it as something women handled among themselves. Indeed, the few records we have on the subject from male medical practitioners suggest that knowledge passed among women in private would have been just as effective, if not more so, than any recommendations from doctors.

Greek physicians mistakenly believed that a woman's most fertile time of the month was just before or after menstruation. Thus, those couples following their doctor's advice and seeking to avoid pregnancy would engage in intercourse during the point of a woman's cycle when she was, in fact, most likely to conceive. This mistaken belief continued for centuries in the face of what must have been overwhelming evidence to the contrary from legions of pregnant women, but male physicians refused to alter their opinion.

Coitus interruptus was also known but depended on the discipline of the male partner to deny himself pleasure at the moment of its greatest height. Thus, it fell to the woman to prevent the man's seed, as it was believed, from taking root in her womb. The Greek physician Soranus recommended that women practice the following to ensure the sperm was expelled: "During intercourse when a man is at the point of orgasm, the woman should hold her breath and shift her position beneath him slightly so that his seed doesn't shoot too far into her uterus. She should then get up immediately and assume a squatting position in which she should make herself sneeze, wipe her vagina all around, and drink something cold."

One Greek physician offered related advice that could reportedly work up to several days after intercourse. One of his female relatives owned a beautiful slave whom she employed as a prostitute and so needed to prevent from becoming pregnant. One day when the slave believed she might have conceived, the doctor told her to jump up and down touching her heals to her buttocks with each leap to shake loose the fertilized egg, which reportedly came out after seven jumps. This story also shows the blurred line between contraception and early-stage abortion in ancient medicine, with pregnancy viewed as a process taking several days rather than the work of a single night.

Various kinds of ointments and physical barriers to pregnancy were also prevalent, such as pastes made out of myrtle oil and white lead and sponges soaked in vinegar, aged olive oil, or honey. Some physicians recommended inserting into the vagina before sex a squirting cucumber, a plant that forcefully expels its own seeds and would presumably do the same to the semen of any man. Other doctors prescribed a meal of beans and water for women in the vain hope that it would prevent pregnancy for up to a year.

Amulets and other magical devices were also popular, as were various sexual activities designed to give a man pleasure without running the risk of pregnancy. If the images from erotic vase paintings are to be taken as evidence, these techniques seem to have been especially in favor with prostitutes whose owners had economic incentives for them not to bear children. Such activities were undoubtedly popular with husbands as well, who were looking for something different from what they would find at home. Paintings show oral, manual, and anal sex acts with prostitutes, none of which would have been thought proper by most wives.

When, in spite of a woman's best preparations, an unwanted pregnancy did result, reasonably effective methods of abortion were available, though the practice was often condemned, at least by men, in ancient times. The famous Hippocratic oath includes a provision by which a physician swears he will not give a woman any medicine to induce an abortion. But this opinion was not held by all doctors, many of whom would employ various drugs and instruments for those women who could afford their high fees.

More cautious physicians warned women that abortions could

be hazardous: "For abortions are more painful than birth since it is not possible to expel the embryo or fetus except through force with drugs, potions, foods, suppositories, or something else. This risks ulcerating or enflaming the womb." Less invasive methods were also available, though of questionable effectiveness. Soranus recommended that a woman wishing to terminate a pregnancy should walk about energetically, jump up and down, and carry heavy objects. Long hot baths and bleeding at the hands of her physician were also prescribed.

The majority of women who could not afford professional medical care to induce an abortion were forced to take matters into their own hands with the painful and dangerous insertion of instruments into the womb or the use of powerful drugs. Many of these women ended up seeking the services of a physician in the end. As one doctor reported: "When, as so often happens with women trying to cure themselves, a woman suffers from a deep wound as a result of an abortion or whose uterus has been damaged by powerful suppositories . . . if she is treated promptly she will regain health but will thereafter be sterile."

The social stigma of abortion also must have discouraged many women from such measures. Women were considered ritually impure for forty days after terminating a pregnancy, and their entire household was thought to be polluted as well. In some Greek cities, a woman who had an abortion after the death of her husband could be charged with a crime and executed, since she was depriving his family of an heir.

Although no evidence suggests that Sappho had to make such a difficult and heartrending decision about a pregnancy herself, the legal and social constraints placed on women in this respect once again reveal how thoroughly men dominated both the private and public aspects of a woman's life, making her achievements even more remarkable.

CARVED IN STONE at the temple of Asclepius at Epidaurus is a story about a young woman named Ithmonica who came to the healing god to seek a child. As was the custom, she lay down in the shrine to sleep, in hope that Asclepius would come to her in a dream. When he appeared, she asked him whether she might conceive a daughter, and he agreed. When the god asked if there was anything else, Ithmonica said she needed nothing more. She became pregnant, but three years later she had still not given birth. Returning to the temple, she asked the god why this was happening to her, but Asclepius said again in a dream that he had given her exactly what she asked for, since she hadn't mentioned anything about actually delivering the child. She then begged the god to let her give birth, and the god agreed. She woke up, left the sanctuary, and gave birth to her daughter in the court-yard outside.

Most pregnancies in ancient Greece undoubtedly were easier than that of poor Ithmonica, but doctors had little understanding of the process, and there were many potential dangers along the way. Physicians were divided on whether the fetus slowly became more human inside the womb as the months passed or quickly took on its final shape and merely grew larger over time. One medical text claimed that the developing child first began to breathe, then to feed on the mother's blood, followed by movement after several months. Aristotle took the unusual step of experimenting with fertilized chicken eggs and reported that the bird's heart is visible beating after only three days. He thus reasoned that the heart was the first organ to develop in the growing human child.

Males were thought to develop more quickly than females, as they were made from stronger seed, moving in the womb after three months while girls took four. This gender difference was supposedly observable in the mother herself, as she would have a healthy complexion with a male child and a pallid face with a female. Boys were also thought to be carried on the right side of the mother's body, while girls grew instead on the inferior left side.

Women reportedly faced many medical risks during pregnancy, from fevers to an unnatural craving for harmful foods. A mother was thought to be at greatest risk of miscarriage during the first forty days of pregnancy and was advised, among other warnings of risk factors, to avoid stepping over a raven's egg. Aristotle advised pregnant women to exercise and eat well but to avoid salt and wine. Physicians were divided about whether or not pregnant women should avoid sex. Some thought an orgasm could bring on miscarriage, though Aristotle believed intercourse could be beneficial for women until the eighth month of pregnancy.

WHEN SAPPHO GAVE birth to Cleis, it would have been in the women's quarters of her household surrounded by female friends and family members. We don't know the details of this or any other birth in ancient Greece from a woman's point of view, since neither Sappho nor any other woman writer mentions it. This information is also incomplete because it consists of accounts from male physicians, who were normally present only at life-threatening deliveries. If no problems were anticipated in the labor, the men of the household withdrew to their own quarters or left the home altogether. Birth was the business of women.

The date of a child's delivery could hardly be controlled, but the ancient Greeks believed certain days of the month were more auspicious than others. A century before Sappho, the poet Hesiod advised that the sixth, ninth, tenth, and sixteenth of each month were favorable for the birth of boys. Only two days, the ninth and fourteenth, were thought promising for girls.

Midwives were employed to help the expectant mother not just in the hours of delivery, but in the days before and after the birth. A midwife was known as a *maia* ("good mother") or *omphaletomos* ("cord cutter") and was skilled at the medical, psychological, and religious aspects of delivery. She was typically an older woman who had given birth herself and was beyond childbearing years. Midwives were encouraged to be intelligent, respectable, and strong enough to handle the physical demands of bringing a child into the world. The physician Soranus also recommended that they have long, thin fingers and keep their nails well trimmed.

After a midwife was called to the home, she would begin by purifying the birthing room with rituals and prayers to the goddesses of childbirth. Hera, the wife of Zeus, was among these, as was the virgin Artemis, but it was Hera's daughter Eileithyia who was most closely associated with labor. When Alcmene, the mother of Hercules, was ready to give birth, Hera in a jealous spite sent Eileithyia to wait outside the women's quarters of the house and delay the birth by whispering spells and sitting with her legs tightly crossed. A clever old woman attending the birth noticed the stranger in the courtyard and understood then why her mistress was suffering so long in agony. She tricked the goddess into thinking the child had been born and broke the spell so that Hercules could be delivered. Eileithyia was furious and turned the old woman into a weasel. Normally, though, goddesses of birth were thought to be quite sympathetic to women in labor.

When the actual time for delivery came, the midwife and other women present prepared the expectant mother and tried to ease her fears as much as they could. But birth could be a frightening business, especially for the first-time mother. As Medea, a mother twice over, says in a play by Euripides:

> *I would rather stand in battle three times than give birth once.*

Some midwives had the woman stand and hold tightly to a post; others urged the patient to lie down in bed. But as one woman in labor was claimed to have said: "Why would I want to go to bed? That's how I got into this mess in the first place!"

The most common position for delivery was sitting on a stool or birthing chair—a technique that allowed gravity to aid in the delivery. In representations in Greek art, we see the laboring mother sitting half-naked in such a chair with her hair loose as she is supported by assistants on either side. If a birthing seat was not available, a woman might sit in the lap of another woman, who would hold her tightly.

A midwife would apply a variety of lubricating ointments for easier delivery. Aristotle believed that the birth of baby boys was more painful and difficult than that of girls, on the reasonable grounds that boys tended to be larger. But boy or girl, an experienced midwife stood ready with the tools needed to handle any contingency of birth. These included olive oil, hot water, sponges, wool, bandages, soothing perfumes for the mother, and a pillow for the newborn infant.

If the delivery became protracted, a midwife could employ several techniques to speed things up, such as shaking the woman up and down, wrapping her genital area tightly in a blanket, or having the mother-to-be lie facedown on a couch while the women present grabbed her legs and pulled them to encourage the child to come out. Correct breathing was also said to help, as was induced sneezing and eating small portions of wolf meat.

When at last the baby was delivered, the women let loose a shout of joy. The midwife would then cut the umbilical cord at a distance of four fingers from the baby's belly with a piece of broken glass or a potsherd. Iron knives were thought to be ill-omened for this important ritual. The exhausted mother and newborn child were then bathed in pure water drawn from a spring, if available, both for cleansing and to begin removing the ritual pollution that was believed to be caused by childbirth. For this act, some physicians recommended wine (as was the custom in Sparta) or the urine of a young child. Visitors would have been discouraged by the religious impurity associated with birth.

Not all births went well, for either the mother or the child. The maternal mortality rate is difficult to determine, but as many as one in ten women may have died in childbirth. In Sparta these women were listed as heroes along with men who fell in battle. In Athens as well, they were honored with tombstones showing them in labor. In many instances it seems the Greeks had no viable way to deal with difficult births. Cesarean sections were practiced, but only as a last resort, since the risk to the mother through blood loss and infection was enormous. When a child could not be delivered whole, the midwife usually resorted to the grisly and dangerous technique of dismembering the child in utero to allow the mother to give birth. The gruesome details of the procedure, described in an ancient medical text, do not make pleasant reading. As an alternative, the physician Soranus recommended using hooks inserted into the obstructed child's body to forcibly pull it from the womb, a procedure that must have put the mother at great risk and left the baby, if it survived, in a condition that would have made it a likely candidate for exposure.

When a birth was successful, there was great joy in the household, and the new mother, above all, was grateful to the gods for a healthy child. It was the custom soon after the birth to thank the goddesses of childbirth by making an offering of clothing worn during the delivery. One third-century-BC inscription by a new father and mother shows that men, too, were full of gratitude for the birth of a child: "The son of Cichesias dedicates these sandals to you, Lady Artemis, and Themistodice dedicates these folded woolen garments, because you came gently to her without your bow when she was in labor and held your hands above her." Such acts of devotion must have been common in Sappho's age as well. A healthy child meant new life for the family and community that all would celebrate.

But in the days after the delivery, when the excitement of the birth was over and the midwife had gone home, the reality of the radical change in her life would have become very real to the first-time mother. In spite of the help she would receive from other women, the endless work of motherhood was now about to begin.

IN A PASSAGE by the historian Xenophon, a grown son complains about his overbearing mother, only to be roundly condemned by Socrates:

> It's the woman who becomes pregnant, carries the child, risks her life for it and gives it nourishment from her own body. Then when she has brought it into the world with difficult labor, she feeds it and cares for it even though she gets no benefit. The infant doesn't know who is helping it and has no way of clearly expressing its desires. Still, the mother tries to guess what it needs and wants and tries to satisfy it, toiling through the days and nights never knowing if she'll someday receive thanks in return.

Aside from this laudatory statement and a few others, ancient Greek literature—even that by Sappho and other women—has very little to say about the life and work of mothers. Like childbirth, it was an area few male writers cared about and reflects a general disinterest by men in what they considered women's work. This leaves us with severely limited sources on what it was like to be a mother in Sappho's world. But one window into motherhood is provided by a scant selection of surviving pieces of ancient Greek art. These images are as rare as literary references, but they have the advantage of providing an actual pictorial glimpse into the daily life of mothers and their children.

One such image is from a slender fifth-century-BC oil vase that shows a harried mother holding a sleeping infant in her left arm while a little boy tugs at her robe. Both the mother and the older child look off apprehensively to their right. At the woman's feet is a basket for wool, while hanging on the wall behind her is a storage sack. This picture shows a wife inside the women's quarters of her household in her two primary roles, as caretaker of children and weaver of clothing. On the opposite side of the vase is a seated man talking with a woman holding a hand mirror. The images may be unconnected, but it's also possible that this is the husband and father conversing with a prostitute while his wife cares for their children.

Another vase from the same century shows a mother encouraging her baby boy to crawl to her across the floor. She stands at the right of the image, bent forward slightly with arms outstretched to her son. The baby has pulled himself up on his arms and looks up at his mother with excitement. In the background is a man, probably the father, observing the scene but not directly involved in the action. As must have been the case with most Greek fathers, he leaves the business of caring for and training young children to their mother.

A small Athenian terra-cotta figurine from the fourth century BC is a rare image of a young girl just a few months old. The chubby toddler has her left leg bent up and her arms outstretched as she sits and looks upward, demanding to be picked up by someone who is likely her mother. Her impatience to be taken care of *now* would be familiar to a parent in any age.

One of the most charming and intimate portraits of a mother and child is depicted on a fine Athenian cup from the fifth century BC. It shows a well-dressed young woman seated on a stool smiling as she reaches out to her infant in a high chair with holes cut out for legs that probably does double duty as a potty seat. The child reaches out to her at the same instant and even lifts its right leg in eagerness. The portrait is a snapshot of an intimate moment, seldom seen in ancient art, when loving mother and child are oblivious to the world around them and absorbed only in each other. The cup was found in the tomb of a wealthy family and may depict a mother who passed away while her child was still young.

Finally, a fifth-century-BC terra-cotta figurine from Boeotia in central Greece shows a mother and daughter at a slightly later stage of childhood and is a unique look at a mother teaching her young daughter to cook. The mother sits in front of a kettle used for heating soup positioned on a low tripod above a fire. The mother leans over the pot to place herbs and spices into it with

Athenian bowl showing a mother and a baby in a high chair (c. 470 BC).

(MUSÉES ROYAUX D'ART ET D'HISTOIRE, BRUSSELS)

her right hand, but at the same time she raises her other hand to warn her daughter to be careful of the hot kettle. The girl has her left hand on her mother's arm for reassurance as she peeks into the boiling pot.

Although mothers were the primary caregivers for their children in ancient Greece, most wealthy families, such as Sappho's, would have employed a nursemaid to help with a child. Many of these women would have been slaves bought specifically for the purpose of child care. Often they were mothers themselves and skilled at the endless chores of child rearing. If they had given birth recently, they would have been employed to nurse the mother's child on occasion and give their mistress a much-needed rest. These women often remained in the household their whole lives and became beloved members of the family, such as Eurycleia, the faithful old nursemaid who serves Penelope in the *Odyssey*. Another such nursemaid, in Aeschylus's *Libation Bearers*, looks back on a boy now grown and gives a picture of infant care that still rings true today:

> Oh, my dear Orestes, I devoted my life to that child from the moment his mother gave him to me to nurse as a newborn babe. He kept me up night after night with his screaming and crying. Such a fuss he made, and all for nothing. Babies are senseless things, you know. You have to care for them like they were little animals and follow their moods. They can't tell you what's the matter, whether they're hungry or thirsty or have soiled themselves. Babies can't control their emotions, it just comes out and there's nothing you can do about it. You do learn to guess in my line of work, but by the gods I was wrong often enough. Then I had to wash his clothes—nurse and laundry woman rolled into one I was.

Aside from a nursemaid, the mother would have had some help from her husband's mother, who ruled as matron of the house, but the relationship between the young wife and her mother-in-law could be fraught with tension. When a new bride moved into her husband's family home, as was the custom, she had to submit to the authority of her mother-in-law. This woman would have been much older than her, with great experience in running the household. She likely held the loyalty of the servants and the love of her son, who would have naturally supported his mother in any quarrels with his wife. Doubtless there were many cases in which a daughter-in-law and her husband's mother got along well, but it wasn't until the mother-in-law died, usually years in the future, that a wife came into her own. Life must have been easier for a young woman once she bore children, especially sons, but the potential for conflict was ever present. If Sappho did indeed give birth to only a single daughter, her relationship with her husband's mother may not have been a pleasant one, though she never mentions it in her surviving poetry.

The relationship between a mother and her children as they grew into adolescence and beyond remained close. Sons would move out of the women's quarters at about the age of six, but they were never far from their mother's care and supervision. Daughters, on the other hand, resided among the women of the house until the day of their marriage. The loss of a child to illness or accident was every mother's greatest fear, and many heartbreaking inscriptions on gravestones commemorate the tragic death of a child before his or her time. One such tombstone tells the story of a mother named Xenoclea who could not bear the death of her son:

Leaving two young daughters, Xenoclea, daughter of Nicarchus, lies here dead. She mourned the sad death of her son Phoenix who died at sea when he was eight years old. There are none so unfeeling of grief, Xenoclea, that they do not pity your fate. You left behind two little girls and died of grief for your son, who has a lonely tomb where he lies in the dark sea.

Like all mothers, those in ancient times worried about their children as they grew older and left home. One fragmentary papyrus letter found in Oxyrhynchus, Egypt, preserves the words of mother to her son Ptolemaeus as he pursues his studies far away:

... hurry and write to me about what you need ... I took care to write your teacher and ask about your health and what you were studying. .... Your sisters send many greetings as do the children—evil eye be gone!—of Theonis and all of our friends.

It shouldn't be supposed that fathers were uncaring about their children. Once boys had passed the early years of childhood, fathers were usually quite involved in raising and educating their sons. Daughters were dear to most fathers as well, even though girls were primarily the responsibility of the mother. A father's love for his daughter is seen clearly in an idealized but quite believable scene in Homer's *Odyssey*, when young Nausicaa approaches her father, King Alcinous, and asks for a cart so that she can supposedly wash laundry at the river—though, in fact, she intends to spend a day at the beach with her girlfriends:

> *She stepped up close to him and spoke confidingly, "Daddy dear,*
>> *I wonder, won't you have them harness a wagon for me,*
>> *the tall one with the smooth wheels,*
>> *so I can take our clothes to the river for washing?*
>> *They are beautiful garments, but they do need a good cleaning.*
>> *And you're so busy sitting among the princes and debating in counsel.*
>> *You really should be wearing spotless linen . . .*

And like any father of a teenage daughter, Alcinous knows well what his daughter is up to, but indulges her anyway.

A mother's relationship with her children did not end at their marriage, but continued to the end of her life, as we will see with Sappho and Cleis. A son was responsible for the care of his mother when his father died, and the evidence we have shows that most sons assumed the task gladly. A man's mother would live with him and his wife until the day she died, all the while enjoying the affection of her son and at least the tolerance of her daughter-in-law. A mother's bond with her daughter also did not end when the girl married, unless her new husband took the daughter far away. Most mothers and grown daughters would have lived in the same area and seen each other regularly during visits to each other's homes and at religious festivals. A mother would be present at the birth of her daughter's children, as Sappho surely would have been at the birth of any children of Cleis, and would rejoice in welcoming a new generation of her family into the world.

4

FAMILY MATTERS

ANTIGONE: *Will you help my hand to lift up the dead?*

ISMENE: *You mean bury him? To go against the law?*

ANTIGONE: *To bury my brother? Yes, and bury yours if you*
will not help me. No one will call me faithless.

ISMENE: *But Creon has forbidden it! You would not dare.*

ANTIGONE: *No one has a right to keep me from my family.*

– SOPHOCLES, *ANTIGONE*

As much as marriage and motherhood defined a woman in Sappho's world, the ties to the family of her birth remained strong throughout a woman's life. Her father was her protector as long as he lived, her mother her adviser and advocate, her sisters her closest friends, and her brothers her childhood companions who stood with her to defend her rights and the honor of the family. As in any age, the potential for conflict, especially between siblings, was ever present, but loyalty to one's family and the reciprocal care provided by all members was fundamental to ancient Greek society.

A woman's relationship with her brothers was especially strong, even after they were all grown. In most cases the siblings continued to live in the same town and saw each other regularly at festivals and family gatherings. A woman's husband was usually many years older than she was, often to the point that they were an entire generation apart. Her brothers, on the other hand, were closer to her own age and had grown up with her since she was a small child. Given the restrictions on women in ancient Greek society, a brother was often the only male of her age that a woman would know well and, if the two got along, could call a friend. Add to this the role of a brother as head of a woman's birth family's household in most cases after the father's death, and it's clear that the ties between brother and sister could be quite powerful by both affection and duty.

The classic literary example of the bond between siblings in ancient Greece is the determination by Antigone, in Sophocles's play of the same name, that her brother Polynices have a proper burial even though it has been forbidden by Creon, the ruler of the city of Thebes. Antigone berates her sister, Ismene, for her fear of defying Creon and reminds her that the responsibilities of a sister to her brother supersede any law made by a man. Antigone is willing to die herself to guarantee a decent burial for Polynices and indeed brings about the death of almost every main character in the play in her relentless quest to fulfill her duty to her brother. As with any example from drama, we can't necessarily believe that this portrayal represents a universal attitude among the Greeks, and some in the audience would have thought Antigone was going too far, but the underlying theme of devotion to family above the state would have resonated deeply with anyone watching the play.

Brothers could be equally devoted to their sisters. When the Athenian tyrant Hipparchus, a few decades after Sappho, was insulted at the rejection of his sexual advances by the handsome young man Harmodius, Hipparchus invited Harmodius's younger sister to be part of a grand procession of maidens in honor of the goddess Athena and then publicly withdrew his invitation, implying that the sister was not a virgin. This insult to his sister and family honor was so great that Harmodius and his relative Aristogiton killed Hipparchus, though it meant death for them both. Many other examples illustrate devotion of grown brothers to their sisters in ancient Greece that go beyond family honor—so far beyond that it's hard not to believe that the bond between brothers and sisters forged in the childhood home remained one of the strongest a woman would know throughout her life.

But just as siblings could be each other's greatest supporters, they could also be bitterly critical when they felt they had been wronged or when a brother or sister was perceived to be harming the interest of the family. The *Works and Days*, composed by the poet Hesiod in the century before Sappho, is set as a sermon from Hesiod to his brother, Perses, who had apparently cheated Hesiod out of his inheritance. The poet presents himself as a poor shepherd tending his flock in the harsh mountains while his brother enjoys the company of rich and corrupt men. Whatever the truth in Hesiod's particular case, fights over money and inheritance were apparently at the root of as many family disputes in ancient Greece as they are today. In Sappho's own poetry, we have ample evidence that a disagreement with a brother over money and family honor led to one of the most painful episodes in her life.

THE PAPYRUS FROM Oxyrhynchus containing a short poetic biography of Sappho records: "She had three brothers, Erigyius, Larichus, and Charaxus, the eldest, who sailed to Egypt and associated with a woman named Doricha and spent large amounts of money on her." The Byzantine *Suda* encyclopedia says even less: "She had three brothers, Larichus, Charaxus, and Erigyius."

A badly damaged Oxyrhynchus papyrus written in the first or second century AD may mention all three brothers, though the text is so damaged it's hard to be sure:

> *Cha(raxus) . . .*
> *and . . .*
> *dearest . . . (Lari)chus . . .*
> *(Eri)gyius for his clothes.*
> *This shows that she was a good housekeeper*
> *and hard worker . . .*
> *as Sappho says in a poem about her brothers . . .*

Aside from the claim that Sappho was industrious around the house, the most interesting statement in this broken fragment is that Sappho wrote a poem about her brothers—a poem, as we will see later, that may have been recently rediscovered. We can say nothing about Sappho's brother Erygius, but the little we know about Larichus does open a window into an important and fascinating aspect of Sappho's life—the volatile and often violent political world of ancient Lesbos.

As mentioned previously, Sappho thought very highly of Larichus, according to the classical writer Athenaeus: "The lovely Sappho often praises her brother Larichus because he poured wine in the town hall for the Mytilenaeans." The role of wine pourer or cupbearer in the ancient world was one of great honor and political importance. As an ancient commentator on Homer's *Iliad* writes: "It was the custom, as Sappho says, for well-born and handsome young men to pour wine." A cupbearer, among his other duties, was trusted to guard the king or ruler from poison, as Nehemiah did for the Persian King Artaxerxes in the Bible. In the Lesbos of Sappho's time, the role would have been less grand than in the court of the great king of Persia, but it still would have been a position of honor that demonstrated Larichus was a trusted adviser of the ruler at Mytilene. By extension, it shows that Sappho's family was in a position of power and high regard at the time Larichus was cupbearer.

We don't know all the details about the political history of Lesbos before and during the life of Sappho, but what we do know reads like family rivalries, power struggles, and betrayal right out of a Shakespearean tragedy. In the Archaic period, the island of Lesbos was divided into at least five competing cities, including Eresus in the west, the likely birthplace of Sappho, and Mytilene in the east, the most powerful of the island's towns. In Sappho's youth, the family of the Penthilidae, who claimed descent from Homer's King Agamemnon, ruled in Mytilene with an iron hand. Like many oligarchies, they maintained power through patronage, control of resources, and the violent crushing of any threats to their power. But at some point in the late seventh century BC, the enemies of the Penthilidae had enough and rose up against the family with a man named Megacles at their lead. Aristotle says Megacles and his armed followers slew the Penthilidae while the latter were beating people with clubs.

Megacles quickly disappears from the scene, but a populist ruler (*tyrannos*, or "tyrant" in Greek) named Melanchros took over Mytilene for a short time until the noble families overthrew and killed him. The leading families of the town then formed an aristocratic faction that shared power for a number of years. The leader of this group was a portly man named Pittacus, son of Hyrras, who came to be known as one of the greatest wise men and lawgivers of ancient Greece. Others in the ruling circle included Antimenidas and Kikis, two elder brothers of the poet Alcaeus, Sappho's contemporary.

At this time, Athens was beginning to flex its overseas muscles and attacked the city of Sigeum near Troy in a bid to control the lucrative trade through Hellespont to the Black Sea. Lesbos saw the attack as a blatant intrusion into its sphere of influence and so fought against Athens, losing at first, but then defeating the Athenians, at least for a time. Pittacus distinguished himself in the war by killing, in single combat, one of the Athenian generals, a great Olympic athlete named Phrynon. In the end,

Athenian calathos-psykter with the Lesbian poets
Alcaeus and Sappho (c. 480 BC).

(STAATLICHE ANTIKENSAMMLUGEN UND GLYPTOTHEK, MUNICH)

however, Athens won control of Sigeum and weakened the hold of Lesbos and the Aeolian Greeks on trade in the region. Unrest spread in Mytilene, and a new populist leader named Myrsilus, of the Cleanactidae clan, arose. But instead of fighting him, Pittacus broke with the other ruling families and swore allegiance to the new tyrant. He further alienated the nobility by marrying a daughter of the Penthilidae, the old aristocratic clan that had ruled Mytilene by force when Alcaeus and Sappho were young.

The poet Alcaeus was furious at this perceived treachery and thereafter delighted in cursing and vilifying Pittacus in his poetry:

> *But Potbelly didn't take these matters to heart.*
> *He trampled his oaths under his feet*
> *and now devours our city . . .*

Alcaeus and his party plotted against Myrsilus and Pittacus but failed and fled to the town of Pyrrha in central Lesbos. Soon, however, they succeeded in overthrowing and perhaps killing Myrsilus and returned in triumph to Mytilene. But once there, they found that the people of the city had rallied to Pittacus and elected him ruler. Alcaeus was livid that the common people would prefer having another so-called tyrant to being ruled by the noble families, but there was nothing the aristocracy could do. Those who opposed Pittacus fled for their lives to distant lands. Alcaeus went to Egypt, while his brother Antimenidas went to Babylon and fought as a mercenary in the army of Nebuchadnezzar, perhaps helping to sack Jerusalem.

Pittacus devoted himself to reforming the government of Lesbos and was greatly admired in later ages for his prudence and wisdom. One of his famous rulings doubled the penalty for crimes committed while drunk—one share of the penalty for breaking the law and the second for being foolish enough to become inebriated in the first place. As sensible as his governance was, the exiles didn't give up, but gathered abroad to nurse their wounds and plot their return to power. They managed to persuade Croesus of Lydia to finance one last campaign against Pittacus, but it failed, and Alcaeus was captured. What must have stung the poet even more than defeat was that Pittacus didn't consider him worth the trouble of executing. Alcaeus, beaten at last, lived out the rest of his life quietly, while Pittacus ruled for ten more years before voluntarily retiring.

How do Sappho, her brother Larichus, and the rest of her family fit into this age of revolution and turmoil in Lesbos? Sappho's own poetry provides a few important clues. A small papyrus fragment unearthed at Oxyrhynchus contains parts of a poem that she wrote against a woman who must have once been her friend:

> . . . *Mica*
> . . . *I will not allow you*
> . . . *you chose the love of the house of Penthilus*
> . . . *evil betrayer*
> . . . *sweet song*
> . . . *voice like honey*
> . . . *gentle breezes*
> . . . *wet with dew*

The house of Penthilus, or the Penthilidae, was the family that had ruled Lesbos when Sappho was a child and had been overthrown. Pittacus had later married a daughter of the clan to strengthen his hold on power after exiling the faction of Alcaeus from the island. This fragment gives us a clear idea of which side Sappho and her family took in the conflict; they were supporters of the noble families who, along with Alcaeus, had sided against the populist Pittacus and his followers. Sappho's sense of betrayal by Mica is palpable in the poem: "you *chose* the love of the house of Penthilus" over loyalty to the party supported by Sappho's family. Mica was certainly not alone in her family's practical choice of reconciliation with Pittacus, but Sappho and her clan must have held Mica and her kin in disdain for selling out so cheaply rather than facing exile as they did.

The best evidence from Sappho's poetry of the price she paid in exile is again from the oldest of her surviving poems, the song contained in the two third-century-BC papyrus fragments from Milan and Copenhagen:

> *But for you, Cleis, I have no beautiful headband*
> *nor do I know how to get one.*
> *But the one in Mytiline . . .*
>
> *. . . to have*
> *. . . adorned*
>
> *. . . these things of the family of Cleanax*

. . . exile

. . . memories dreadfully wasted away

Here, once again, is the sorrow Sappho feels at not being able to provide a suitable headband for her daughter Cleis, as her mother had done for her in the days before Pittacus—probably "the one in Mytiline"—drove the family from Lesbos. What "these things of the family of Cleanax" are is missing, but the hostile reference is clear. They were the family of Myrsilus, whom Pittacus swore loyalty to at the expense of the nobility that must have included Sappho's clan.

Political comments in Sappho's poems are rare, but they do illustrate something quite remarkable. The poetry of her contemporary Alcaeus is brimming with deprecations against Pittacus and his allies, but we would scarcely expect a woman to comment on such matters. Sappho is rightly known as a poet of love, but these two poems show that she was very much interested in politics and protested against the wrongs she felt had been done to her family in perhaps the only way available to her, with the power of her songs. These poems, like the best political satire, have a bite that the endless protests and plotting of men could never achieve.

Sappho and her family probably shared the first displacement of the opponents of Pittacus in Pyrrha on Lesbos, but her second and more lengthy exile was on the distant island of Sicily south of Italy. The Parian Marble, a chronology of early Greek history from an inscription in stone found on the Aegean island of

Paros, records that Sappho fled to Sicily sometime around the year 600 BC. The Greeks had begun to settle in Sicily more than a century before Sappho's birth, and by her time they had many prosperous colonies on its shores—so many that it became a kind of second Greece in the classical age.

Sappho and her family would have had many choices of where on the island to settle in exile. One possibility was Panormus (modern Palermo) on the northwest coast, though this city was ruled by the Carthaginians. Sappho mentions Panormus in one of her fragments, but this is no strong argument that she lived there. A better guess would be Syracuse on the east coast. This prosperous town had been founded by Corinth a century earlier and had strong commercial ties to the Aegean. We know from the first-century-BC Roman orator Cicero that a celebrated statue of Sappho was on prominent display in the town hall of Syracuse before it was stolen by the greedy Roman governor Verres, though again this is not solid proof that the poet lived there more than four hundred years earlier.

In the end, we are again left with many questions. That Sappho was as active politically as a woman could be in her age is certain, as is the alliance of her family with other nobles against Pittacus, a man they perceived as a feckless traitor to his own class. Sappho and her family paid the price of exile in distant Sicily, likely for several years, before they were presumably allowed to return to Lesbos after their humiliating final defeat by Pittacus. The service of her brother Larichus as cupbearer in the town hall could have occurred at any point before the family's exile when Pittacus had allied himself with Myrsilus and then became ruler of Mytilene by popular vote. What became of Larichus afterward, or whether he even survived the final uprising against Pittacus, is unknown.

SAPPHO'S WORLD WAS small compared to the world we know today. In her poems she mentions the Greek islands and mainland; the coast of Asia Minor, along with the kingdoms of Lydia and Phrygia just to the east; Scythia beyond the Black Sea to the north; and the large Mediterranean islands of Cyprus and Sicily. She certainly knew about Egypt as well, and the Mesopotamian empires of Assyria and Babylon. Beyond these lands her picture of the world probably grew unclear.

She may have known about the land of the Ethiopians to the south of Egypt and something of western Arabia, where frankincense and myrrh were gathered. She could have heard stories about the rich kingdoms of India on the trade routes to the east, and it's just possible that tales of the Seres, or silk people, of distant China could have reached the shores of Lesbos by her day. To the west she would have known about Italy and the coasts of Spain and Gaul, which were being settled by Greek colonists in her lifetime. She also could have heard from Phoenician and Greek traders about the great, unending ocean beyond Spain, where the tin-rich island of Britain lay and, on the edge of the world, Ierne, or Ireland, rumored to be a land of cannibals.

We know that Lesbos had a lively trade with the lands of the eastern Mediterranean in Sappho's time. Large transport jars for wine and oil called amphorae were one of the chief exports of Lesbos and are regularly unearthed by archaeologists around the Mediterranean. One of the earliest examples of these jars comes from a coastal fortress near Tel Aviv in Israel dating to the decades before Sappho. Lesbos, in turn, imported fine pottery and other trade items from mainland Greece and Asia Minor, many of which have been recently discovered in excavations at Mytilene and elsewhere on the island. We've already seen that Lesbos fought with Athens in Sappho's lifetime to control the lucrative trade into the Black Sea and beyond. According to the testimony of archaeological and literary sources, including Sappho's own poetry, Lesbos was a vibrant, wealthy, and outward-looking trade center well placed between Greece and the rich lands to the east and north.

The references we find in Sappho to other cities and countries are few, but they provide some of our most important literary evidence for trade connections during this period. She mentions the nearby port of Phocaea and its luxury wares in one of her poems recorded by the writer Athenaeus:

> . . . *hand cloths*
> . . . *purple*
> . . . *sent from Phocaea*
> . . . *expensive gifts*

Phocaea lay on the coast of Asia Minor only a day's sail south of Lesbos. Its lands were poor for agriculture, so the citizens of the city had turned to maritime trade. About 600 BC, they founded the colony of Massalia (modern-day Marseilles) near the mouth of the Rhône River in Gaul to profit from merchant goods coming down the river from the Celtic lands of central Europe. The Phocaeans also founded colonies in Corsica and along the Mediterranean coast of Spain, and they had extensive dealings with the Tartessians on the Atlantic coast of Iberia beyond the Pillars of Hercules. The close connections between Lesbos and Phocaea could have opened many doors for trade and profit for the aristocracy of the island, including Sappho's family.

Sappho also sang of longing for goods from Lydia in Asia Minor to give to her daughter Cleis during her exile, indicating trade connections to the east, as well as the first references in Greek literature to incense from southern Arabia. But it's Sappho's stinging poems about her brother Charaxus, who traded in Egypt, that are the most interesting foreign connection in her poetry.

Egypt was the oldest center of civilization in the Mediterranean and had long been known to the Greeks. By the time of Sappho, the pyramids were almost as ancient to her as she is to us, but the possibilities for wealth from trade with this land on the bountiful Nile were undiminished and drew many merchants and adventurers from the Aegean and beyond. During the reign of Pharaoh Psammetichus I, who came to power in the seventh century BC with the help of Greek mercenaries, the trading city of Naucratis was founded on the westernmost branch of the Nile.

Naucratis was a town settled and run by Greeks, especially from the Aegean islands, including citizens from Mytilene on Lesbos. There the Greek residents built temples to Zeus, Hera, and Apollo and operated the port as a center of trade between

Greece and the Egyptian heartland to the south. The Greeks exported wine, oil, grain, silver, pottery, and perhaps slaves to the Egyptians, while the Egyptians exported back to Greece linen, papyrus, ivory, and other exotic goods. As with ports and trading centers in any century, the bustling town of Naucratis was full of lonely men with money in their pockets and soon became a leading center for the world's oldest profession. Among the clients of the high-class prostitutes in the city was Charaxus, Sappho's brother.

The first poem of Sappho that the Oxford archaeologists Grenfell and Hunt found at the garbage dump of ancient Oxyrhynchus was a fragmentary prayer and biting satire against her brother Charaxus:

> *. . . Nereids, grant that*
> *my brother come back to me unharmed*
> *and that all he wishes for in his heart*
> *comes true.*

> *And grant that he atone for all his past mistakes.*
> *Make him a joy to his friends and a grief*
> *to his enemies. And may no one bring us sorrow*
> *ever again.*

> *May he wish to bring honor*
> *to his sister, but dismal grief . . .*
> *. . . sorrowing before*
> *. . . listening, millet seed*

. . . of the citizens
. . . not again
. . . but you, Cypris
. . . putting aside evil

The most striking thing about this poem is that Sappho would air her family's problems so openly. It's possible this was a private composition meant only for Charaxus, but the fact that it survived the ages implies that it was circulated to some degree on Lesbos. Family shortcomings were not commonly discussed outside the household, since anything one member did made the rest look bad. To advertise the sins of Charaxus meant that Sappho was so incensed by her brother's behavior (and had presumably exhausted quieter means of correcting him) that she was willing to write a satire against him for others to hear. It's an extraordinary look into the frustration of a sister against her brother because of the shame that he'd brought on the family.

Sappho deliberately begins in this poem with a reverent and hopeful stanza asking the gods to look after Charaxus, help him to return safely to Lesbos from his voyage abroad, and grant him his heart's desire. It's only with the first line of the second stanza that she twists the knife:

And grant that he atone for all his past mistakes.

Charaxus has brought great sorrow and grief to his family, but Sappho doesn't give us details until the third stanza, when she claims that he has brought dishonor to her as his sister. Then the

poem breaks off into scattered surviving words and phrases—
"sorrowing," "dismal grief," "putting aside evil"—that make us
long to know what was said in the missing fragments. How the
millet seed fits into the song is anyone's guess.

In another early and even more incomplete fragment found
at Oxyrhynchus, Sappho gives us the name of the woman who
has led her brother astray:

> *of Doricha . . .*
> *commands, for not . . .*
> *arrogance . . .*
> *for young men . . .*
>   *beloved . . .*

And in another poem she speaks of Doricha with language simi-
lar to the earlier prayer:

> *. . . that he atone for his past mistakes*
> *. . . with fortune of the harbor*
> *. . . Cypris, and may she find you very harsh.*
> *And may she—that Doricha—not boast, saying*
> *he came a second time*
>   *to her longed-for love.*

We know from later commentators that Doricha, also called
Rhodopis, was born in the wild land of Thrace across the north-
ern Aegean Sea from Lesbos. She was reportedly a slave—along
with Aesop, the famous author of fables—owned by a man from

Mytilene named Iadmon. And lest we cast Doricha too quickly as the villain in this tale, we should keep in mind that she was a sex slave forced into prostitution by a man who wanted to profit from her use and degradation by male clients against her will.

The historian Herodotus has an alternate version of the story, saying that Doricha was owned by a man named Xanthes from the island of Samos to the south of Lesbos and was brought by him to Egypt to ply her trade. The Greek geographer Strabo confirms that Doricha was a mistress of Charaxus, whom he describes as a merchant exporting Lesbian wine to Naucratis. The writer Athenaeus also relates that a poem written by Posippus says:

> Doricha, your bones fell asleep long ago . . .
> the bands of your hair, your perfumed shawl
> in which you once wrapped Charaxus
> and joining him to your body
> you grasped the wine cup in the small hours.

The fact that her brother had a dalliance with a prostitute would not have bothered Sappho or any of the upright citizens of Mytilene. Such affairs were common and expected of men, whether single or married. It's what Charaxus did next that caused such grief and shame to Sappho and her family. Not content to visit Doricha and take his pleasure with her on distant shores, he purchased her at great cost to the family and brought her back to Lesbos. Once home, he continued to spend lavishly on her, and then fathered children with her. This was simply too much for Sappho. Not only had Charaxus wasted the family's resources to buy a prostitute's freedom, but he had brought her back to their hometown, where he had had offspring with her. If he had actually married Doricha, their children might have been legitimate heirs of the family fortune. In the context of the world in which they lived, the shame this would have brought to Sappho and her family merited the unusual step of public satire against her brother.

There is a hint of the final chapter of the Doricha affair in the Roman poet Ovid's *Letters of the Heroines*, a later and mostly fictional work that may nonetheless have some basis in poems of Sappho that are now lost. Ovid puts the words of the poem in the mouth of Sappho, who says that her brother was captured by love and endured shameful financial losses, after which he was reduced to poverty and roamed the sea as a common brigand. If there's any truth to the tale, it was a sad end for the third and last of Sappho's brothers.

UNTIL RECENTLY, THIS was all we could say about Sappho and her siblings. But in 2014, a previously unknown Sappho poem was revealed to the world that sheds new light on her family relations. Dr. Dirk Obbink of Oxford University, one of the world's leading experts on ancient papyri, was contacted by an anonymous owner residing in London who had acquired papyrus fragments containing not one but two new poems by Sappho. The poems were copied by a professional scribe in the early Christian era; then later, when the texts were worn, the papyrus was probably recycled as book bindings. The poems lay unread for centuries and then in the 1950s were sold by a Cairo antiquities dealer to a professor at the University of Mississippi. The poems remained there hidden amid a mass of papyrus fragments until they were sold by the university in the 1980s to finance the purchase of papers of the novelist William Faulkner, a native son of the state. The fragments containing the still-undiscovered poems were finally sold at auction in London to the collector, who contacted Dr. Obbink for help in identifying what he had bought. Only then did the lost poems come to light.

The second of the two poems is a short, fragmentary prayer to Aphrodite, but the first is a remarkably well-preserved poem of five Sapphic stanzas concerning her brothers Charaxus and Larichus. This exciting discovery has been christened "The Brothers Poem" and joins only a handful of complete or near-complete songs by Sappho. There is still much controversy about the correct reading of the poem; a preliminary translation follows:

But you are always chattering that Charaxus is coming
with a full ship. These things, I suppose, Zeus
knows and all the other gods. But you should not
   worry about them.

Instead send me and ask me to call on
and make many prayers to Queen Hera
that Charaxus return here,
   steering his ship,

and find us safe and sound. Everything else,
all of it, let us leave to the gods.
For fair weather comes quickly
      from great storms.

Those to whom the King of Olympus wishes
to send a helpful spirit to banish toils,
these will be happy
      and rich in blessings.

And we—if someday his head is freed from labor
and Larichus becomes a gentleman of leisure—
may we be delivered quickly
      from great heaviness of heart.

This may be the missing poem mentioned in the Oxyrhynchus fragment that Sappho wrote about her brothers, but the song names only two of the three, though at least one stanza is missing at the beginning. It is, however, the first surviving poem composed by Sappho herself that unambiguously names her brothers Charaxus and Larichus. Like the first Sappho poem discovered by Grenfell and Hunt in the garbage dump at Oxyrhynchus, it is a prayer for the safety of her brother.

The poem begins with Sappho chiding an unknown person for always chattering on about Charaxus returning home with a ship full of trade goods. We don't know who this person is, but because Greek endings can identify gender, we do know that it is a woman, perhaps Sappho's mother. The theme of the first part of the poem is that we should trust in the gods and realize that the dangers we face in life are in their hands. The parallels to an ode by the first-century-BC Roman writer Horace are so striking that he may be drawing on Sappho's once-lost poem for inspiration:

> *Leave everything else to the gods,*
> *who quickly calm the battling winds*
> *on the stormy seas . . .*

It is not Poseidon, the god of the seas, that Sappho calls on, but Hera, a goddess, as we have seen, particularly concerned with women. In a beautiful line at the end of the third stanza, Sappho gives us the proverb that "fair weather comes quickly from great storms"—a lesson she suggests that holds for all of life, not just sea voyages.

In the fourth stanza she declares that Zeus, the "King of Olympus," will send a *daimon* to those he wishes to be happy and blessed. This word is the origin of the English "demon," but in Greek it is a positive term referring to a god (as it does in the plural in the third stanza of this poem) or to any other divine spirit. Here it has the more specific meaning of a kind of spiritual guide or, as we might say, guardian angel. Socrates later used the same word to explain that he had a divine spirit that guided him in his life. Sappho says that those who are fortunate enough to be granted this heavenly guardian by Zeus will be *makares*, a word later used by Christians to mark those blessed by God.

In many ways, though, it is the final stanza of this new

poem that is the most interesting. Sappho here shifts her gaze from Charaxus to her favored younger brother Larichus, hoping that he will rise up for the good of the family. The leisure she wishes for her brother is not a negative term but is the affluence and freedom from toil that is the mark of the nobility. If he can achieve this, Sappho says, she (using the plural "we" as she often does) will be freed from her *baruthumia*, a Greek word meaning a weighty depression or heaviness of heart. Sappho, however, isn't clear about what has caused this heaviness. It may be that she simply worries about the dangerous life of her seagoing brother Charaxus, but it's also possible that word of Charaxus's dealings with the prostitute Doricha has already reached Sappho and that here she is praying for Larichus to grow up quickly and set things right for the family. The heaviness of heart could also be due to the family's political troubles with the ruler Pittacus, or it could be caused by something else entirely. Whatever the trouble might be, Sappho is deliberately echoing Homer in this poem, paralleling Charaxus with the roving Odysseus, Larichus with young Telemachus, and featuring herself as the long-suffering Penelope.

It would be helpful if we could know exactly when in Sappho's life the poem was composed. The best guess is that it was fairly early, since Larichus is a young man, but that still leaves a great deal of room for interpretation. Our best hope is that other poems of Sappho await discovery that will fill in the missing pieces of the life of Sappho and her troubled family.

5

LOVING WOMEN

This is why we have an innate love for one another. It brings us back to our original state, trying to reunite and restore us to our true human form. Each of us is only part of a person that was split in two, like half of a tally stick or a filleted fish. We're all looking for our other half.

– PLATO, *SYMPOSIUM*

THERE WAS NO word for "homosexual" in ancient Greek. The very idea that a person could be defined strictly by sexual preference would have seemed strange to most people in classical times. Of course, there were men who preferred men; women, such as Sappho, who preferred women; and those who favored the opposite sex. But the boundaries between the various types of sexual orientation were not as fixed as they are in the modern world. A man might make passionate love with a woman in the afternoon and then spend an intimate evening with a male companion, with no one giving it a second thought. This isn't to say there were no socially accepted rules of sexual behavior or that those who strayed from community standards weren't mocked and condemned. The Greeks considered some sexual acts and inclinations out of bounds, but these standards varied by time and place in a way that is difficult for us to understand, since our evidence is limited and our interpretation so often colored by modern attitudes.

In recent years it has become popular among scholars to view ancient sexual conduct through a male-centered active/passive model. This means that one partner in an intimate relationship was seen as holding the power and being dominant, while the other was literally on the receiving end of the action. To put it somewhat crudely, one person was the penetrator while the other, whether male or female, was the penetrated. This model works well in some ways, but it doesn't begin to capture the complexity of intimate human relations in the classical world, nor does it particularly help us understand sexual relationships between women.

One type of sexual activity in the Greek world was the well-documented pederasty between grown men and adolescent boys in ancient Athens. It was common, at least among the upper classes in that city, for an adult man to take on a teenage youth as a kind of pupil in the arts of life and love. The older man would act as a mentor and provide the boy with gifts and guidance in all manner of social and political matters, while the younger partner would return affection and physical satisfaction within certain accepted bounds. In theory at least, any sort of penetration of the younger man by the older was considered inappropriate, though plenty of drinking cups show scenes of manual and intercrural ("between the thighs") sex between adolescent boys and their sponsors. This sort of same-sex relationship certainly existed, at least in Athens, but the evidence we have from classical times shows a great variety of sexual behaviors between members of the same gender.

Contrary to Athenian pederasty, early poets such as Theognis in the generation after Sappho sang of young men enjoying sex with other males their own age:

> *In youth you can sleep through the night with a friend,*
> *unloading your desire for lusty action.*

And these relationships did not necessarily end at the time of maturity and marriage. As the Greek poet Strato wrote in the Roman era:

> *Although your first down, turning to hair, springs from*
> *you,*
> *and soft blond curls are upon your temples,*
> *I will not abandon my beloved. His beauty is yet my own,*
> *even bearded, even with hair.*

Some grown men even cultivated a feminine appearance as adults so that they would remain attractive to other males, while other pairs of male lovers alternated between active and passive roles. Medical texts recognized that some men, by nature, were attracted to other men throughout their lives and accepted this as normal.

However, we shouldn't suppose that all Greeks approved of male same-sex encounters. The poet Archilochus in the generation before Sappho heaps scorn on such sexual relationships as an upper-class indulgence. Later comedy from Athens viciously lampoons effeminate men and passive sexual partners. And speakers in law courts routinely scored points with a jury by accusing their male adversaries of engaging in sexual affairs with other men. In the cosmopolitan city of Pompeii buried beneath the ash of Mount Vesuvius, there are many examples of vulgar sexual graffiti from throughout the town, most of it derogatory. For example: "Cosmos, the slave of Equitia, is a big pervert and sucks cock with his legs spread apart." One graffito of Jewish or Christian origin compares the whole town of Pompeii to Sodom and Gomorrah.

Acceptance of male same-sex relationships varied in ancient Greece, and the same was true of same-sex relationships between women, though reactions to these are often more negative. Writers, almost all male, generally considered lesbian relations to be contrary to the natural order and beyond the bounds of proper feminine behavior. The third-century-BC writer Asclepiades captures this mood in one of his epigrams:

> *The girls from Samos, Bitto and Nannion, don't want*
> *to meet with Aphrodite on her own terms.*
> *But, Lady Cypris, they desert to other practices—and not*
> *good ones.*
> *Shun these fugitives from your bed.*

Archilochus, who mocked sexual relations between upper-class men, complains about women who don't want to marry men—perhaps an acknowledgment of those who prefer other females or maybe just griping about women who want nothing to do with him. Plutarch, however, is uncondemning when he talks about the women of Sparta, presenting a type of relationship more like the man-boy pairings of Athens: "Love was so esteemed among them that girls became the erotic objects of noble women."

Add to this the evidence of homoerotic bonds between adolescent girls in Alcman's earlier *Maiden Songs* and we may reasonably suppose that Sparta was more liberal than the rest of Greece in accepting female same-sex relationships. The noted physician Hippocrates agreed that some women by nature were drawn to other women, as did Plato in the famous parable of the original human beings—some male, some female, some both—who were split apart by Zeus for their pride and are forever trying to find their missing halves.

The second-century-AD Greek author Lucian writes about an intriguing, though fictional, account of three women, two of whom are involved in a long-term relationship. A friend addresses one of the women, Leaena, the courtesan:

> *We hear interesting things about you, Leaena. Namely that Megilla, that wealthy woman from Lesbos, is in love with you as a man is in love and that you have sexual intercourse with each other, doing I don't know what.*

Leaena confirms the rumors and describes a party she attended with Megilla and the third woman, Demonassa. After that, Megilla and Demonassa invite her to lie between them:

They kissed me like men, not just touching lips but with an open mouth, putting their arms around me and fondling my breasts. . . . Then Megilla removed her wig and revealed a shaven head like the manliest of athletes.

Megilla then declares she doesn't want to be considered as a female that evening, but as the masculine Megillus. She informs Leaena that Demonassa is her wife and they have been married for many years:

I was born a woman like the rest of you women, but my mind and desire and everything else is that of a man.

Leaena begins to describe to her friend the night of passion that followed, but she refrains from the details, saying they are too shameful. Lucian's dialogue may be a male fantasy of a lesbian ménage à trois, or it might reflect some reality of same-sex marriage between women in the ancient world. If so, it seems likely that such marriages had to be hidden, as was the case with Megilla and Demonassa.

Finally, a pair of magic spells surviving from Egypt in early Christian times provides us a rare look at everyday women, revealing their own same-sex desires. The first is from a second-century-AD papyrus that records a spell seeking to draw together two women:

I implore you, Good Messenger, by Anubis and Hermes and all the gods below, attract and bind Sarapias,

daughter of Helen, to this woman Herais, whom
Thermoutharin bore. Now, now—quickly, quickly. . . . By
her soul and heart attract Sarapias.

The second example, of a darker tone, is a slightly later spell inscribed on a lead tablet:

Root of gloomy darkness, jagged-tooth three-headed
dog covered with coiling snakes, traveler in the recesses
of the Underworld—Come, spirit-driver, with
the Furies, savage with their stinging whips. Holy
serpents, maenads, frightful maidens, come to my angry
incantations. . . . By means of this corpse-demon inflame
the heart, the liver, and the spirit of Gorgonia, daughter
of Nilogenia, with love and affection for Sophia, whom
Isara bore. . . . Burn, set on fire, inflame her soul.

Spells like these were commonly used in the ancient world for curses and charms between men and women, but it is exceptional to discover examples of one woman imploring the gods and powers of the underworld to bind another woman to her in a passionate relationship.

A few other Greek women write about intimate connections with their own gender, but most of what we know from a female point of view about same-sex relationships in the ancient world comes, in fact, from Sappho, our earliest and best source on the subject. Her poems of passion for other women are often fragmentary and open to interpretation, but by reading them closely, we can gain not only a better knowledge of lesbian love in Sappho's age, but a deeper appreciation for some of the greatest poetry the human heart has ever composed.

THE ONLY SURVIVING poem of Sappho complete from beginning to end comes by way of the Greek historian and literary critic Dionysius of Halicarnassus, who quotes the poem in full in his book on literary composition:

> *Deathless Aphrodite on your dazzling throne,*
> *child of Zeus, weaver of snares, I pray to you,*
> *do not, with anguish and pain, O Lady,*
> > *break my heart.*
>
> *But come here now, if ever in the past,*
> *listening, you heard my cries from afar*
> *and leaving your father's golden house,*
> > *you came to me,*
>
> *yoking your chariot. Beautiful swift sparrows*
> *drew you over the black earth*
> *with their whirling wings, down from the sky*
> > *through the middle of the air,*
>
> *and quickly they arrived. And you, O Blessed Goddess,*
> *with a smile on your immortal face,*

asked what was the matter now and why
       had I called you again

and what I wanted most of all to happen,
me, with my crazy heart: "Who should I persuade this
       time
to lead you back to her love? Who is it, Sappho,
       who has done you wrong?

For even if she runs away, soon she will pursue.
If she refuses gifts, she'll be giving instead.
And if she won't love, she will soon enough,
       even against her will."

So come to me now, free me from unbearable
pain. All my heart yearns to happen—
make it happen. You yourself,
       be my ally.

The poem is remarkable for a number of reasons, most notably the intensely personal interaction between Sappho and the goddess Aphrodite, but we will look at the tantalizing religious aspects of the song in the next chapter. Here we should focus on what this poem can tell us about Sappho and same-sex love.

No two modern scholars can agree completely on the meaning and significance of the poem, but it is clear to everyone that Sappho is calling on the goddess of love to help her win over a woman she very much desires. The most obvious thing to note is that Sappho herself is part of the song. This isn't the only poem in which the poet sings of her own longings, but it is one of the few in which she names herself, here through the voice of the goddess. Of course, it's possible that Sappho inserted herself as a fictional character in her own poem much as Dante did in the *Divine Comedy* and that she invented the whole scenario of unrequited love as a poetic fiction, but it seems much more likely that the song is a genuine cry from Sappho's own heart. And if anyone doubts the object of her desire is actually a woman, the Greek language makes it clear that the mysterious beloved is a female. Thus we are left with Sappho's only complete poem declaring unequivocally that she herself is deeply, passionately in love with another woman.

Sappho reveals in this poem that she isn't new to the pain and struggles of the heart. As Aphrodite asks Sappho with a weary sigh in the fourth stanza (the original Greek is even better at conveying the humor of the passage), what is the matter *now* and why have you called me *again* to come to your aid? Sappho deliberately portrays herself as an ever-hopeful woman with a "crazy heart" who is consistently unlucky in love, rather like a character from a modern romantic comedy.

Fortunately for Sappho, she has a powerful ally in the goddess of love. Not only does Aphrodite agree to help, but she is going to do it in such a way that the unknown woman will beg Sappho to return. The goddess promises she will make the romance happen even against the other woman's will. She will do this, quite simply, with magic.

Love charms and magic spells, like the two lesbian incantations from Egypt we saw earlier, were quite common in the ancient world. They were inscribed on tablets, written on papyrus, and worn as amulets from Egypt to Britain, all in an effort to win the love of another. The ancients regarded magic and charms of all sorts very highly, and many believed wholeheartedly in their effectiveness. Homer even sings of incantations able to stanch bleeding from wounds. Spells were particularly effective, it was believed, if they used the incantatory power of repeated sounds. Like the hypnotic rhythm of a child's lullaby, an ancient magic charm was at its best when it used carefully composed repetitive patterns.

This is exactly what Sappho does in the sixth stanza of this poem:

> *For even if she runs away, soon she will pursue.*
> *If she refuses gifts, she'll be giving instead.*
> *And if she won't love, she will soon enough,*
> *even against her will.*

Preserved in this poem may be one of the earliest examples of a Greek magic spell, predating most others by centuries. It may seem unfair that Sappho is willing to use enchantment to win the affection of a woman she loves, but in the ancient world it was an accepted practice. It's difficult to know in any case how serious Sappho is about calling on Aphrodite to bend the will of her beloved in such a drastic way. It may be that she is simply adopting a magical formula as a demonstration of her poetic skill, but it could also be, as seems likely, that Sappho is quite sincere in using this charm to conquer the heart of the mysterious woman.

ONE OF SAPPHO'S most striking poems is preserved in an ancient work, called *On the Sublime*, composed by a writer known as Longinus in the first century AD. Only the final part of the poem is missing:

> *He seems to me equal to the gods,*
> *that man who sits opposite you*
> *and listens near*
> > *to your sweet voice*

> *and lovely laughter. My heart*
> *begins to flutter in my chest.*
> *When I look at you even for a moment*
> > *I can no longer speak.*

> *My tongue fails and a subtle*
> *fire races beneath my skin,*
> *I see nothing with my eyes*
> > *and my ears hum.*

> *Sweat pours from me and a trembling*
> *seizes my whole body. I am greener*

than grass and it seems I am a little short
of dying.

But all must be endured, for even a poor man . . .

Fortunately for us, Longinus explains why he chose to quote this particular poem. It is one of the longest and most insightful ancient commentaries on the poetry of Sappho:

> Sappho each time uses the emotions associated with the madness of love from the attendant circumstances and from the thing itself. How does she display this excellence? She does it by combining the most important and powerful feelings that accompany the emotion. . . . Aren't you amazed how in this poem she in the same moment seeks out the soul, body, hearing, tongue, sight, and skin as though they were all something external to her, and how she both freezes and burns, is afraid and nearly dead, so that we see in her not a single emotion but many coming together? All this of course is what happens to people in love. But it is her selection, as I have said, of all the most important features and her combination of them that have produced such an amazing result.

Readers of this poem for two thousand years have agreed with Longinus. Little else in the literature of any age captures the physical sensations of erotic love like Sappho's description of the overwhelming passion she feels for the unnamed woman of the poem. This song is also one of the clearest examples of same-sex love in the poetry of Sappho, though some readers have tried very hard to see it as something else.

Many leading male scholars of the nineteenth and early twentieth centuries wanted desperately to portray Sappho as a proper Victorian lady, preferably as a kind of headmistress at an ancient finishing school for young women. When confronted by such clearly homoerotic poetry as this and the previous poem, they were forced to perform all manner of interpretative contortions to maintain the image of Sappho that they had created. One ingenious solution was to declare that this poem is set at a wedding banquet and that the woman and man sitting opposite each other are bride and groom. In this scenario, Sappho's poem becomes a wedding song in celebration of the perfectly acceptable heterosexual love between this pair. Any passion expressed by the poet who watches them is explained as the feelings of the groom toward his bride expressed through the voice of the poet.

One of the problems with this theory is that nowhere does Sappho mention marriage, nor does she refer to a bride or groom, as she does frequently in her genuine wedding songs. The unnamed man at the beginning of the poem, in fact, disappears almost immediately. What we have instead is a setting no more defined than one in which three people, one man and two women, are sitting near each other at an unknown occasion. It may be a grand banquet or dinner party of some sort, but it could just as easily be three friends resting under a tree. There is also no good reason to suppose that we have here a tormented love triangle. Sappho never says she is jealous of the man, only that she envies him as he sits close to the woman so obviously enjoying his company. The idea that she is jealous has been colored, literally, by the word "greener" in the fourth stanza—a shade not associated with envy or jealousy in the ancient world. What is clear from this poem is that the speaker (who again we know is a woman, thanks to the gendered endings of Greek words) is overwhelmed by intense, erotic feelings.

Anyone who has ever been madly overcome by passion will recognize the symptoms expressed so poignantly by Sappho, what the modern classical scholar Jane McIntosh Snyder so appropriately calls the "raw physicality" of the poem. First her heart begins to flutter. Sappho was not the earliest to employ this motif; Homer uses the same Greek word (*ptoeo*, "to flutter, fly away") to describe the emotions of Penelope's suitors in the *Odyssey*, as does Alcaeus when he says that Helen was overcome by her lover, Paris. This is not just a quaint metaphor, but a physical description of a heart set racing by passion and pounding wildly in the poet's chest.

From the heart, Sappho moves to her weakening tongue, which "fails" (or literally "breaks") as she beholds the woman, using the same word that Homer does when he describes a chariot falling to pieces on the battlefield. Next comes a burning fire rushing beneath her skin, and then blindness strikes her eyes, which just a moment before were so fixed on the woman. Her ears begin to buzz like a *rhombos*, or bull-roarer, a musical instrument whirled around on the end of a string used as a child's toy, but also in religious rites and, intriguingly, as a love charm. Sweat flows down her body like rain, and trembling seizes her, so that Sappho describes herself as "greener than grass" and "a little short of dying"—both phrases that may be more sexually suggestive than they first appear.

Sappho uses the comparative form of the adjective *chloros* (the root of the plant pigment *chlorophyll*) when she says "greener than grass." The word indeed has the meanings "green, greenish-yellow, pale" in ancient Greek, but the classical scholar Eleanor Irwin has made a strong case that in early times it meant "moist" or "wet" when used with plants. If Sappho is using it in this sense, the line could instead be translated "I am wetter than grass." This could refer to sweat, as earlier in the stanza, but it could also mean the vaginal moisture that arises from sexual arousal.

Immediately following this is Sappho's statement that she is "a little short of dying," which again could be hyperbole for being overwhelmed with passion or could refer to *le petit mort* ("the little death")—a long-standing metaphor for orgasm. If this is correct, we can read the poem in a whole new way. In this most erotic of songs, Sappho gazes at the woman she loves and experiences the physical sensations of rapid pulse, breathlessness, inability to speak, hypersensitive skin, dullness of vision, humming in her ears, trembling, sexual lubrication, and finally climax. Victorian scholars would have been scandalized by such an interpretation, but it may well be true.

A PIECE OF parchment from the sixth century AD preserves a different kind of love poem by Sappho. Like many of her songs, the beginning and end are missing, and the middle has many gaps, but we can read enough of the poem to see that it's an emotional dialogue between Sappho and a woman as they say farewell to each other, perhaps forever:

> . . . "I honestly wish I were dead."
> Weeping she left me
>
> with many tears and said this:
> "Oh, this has turned out so badly for us, Sappho.
> Truly, I leave you against my will."
>
> And I answered her:
> "Be happy and go—and remember me.
> for you know how much we loved you.
>
> But if not, I want to remind
> you . . .
> . . . and the good times we had.
>
> For many crowns of violets
> and roses and . . .
> . . . you put on by my side,
>
> and many woven garlands
> made from flowers
> around your soft throat,

and with much perfume
costly . . .
fit for a queen, you anointed yourself.

And on a soft bed
delicate . . .
you let loose your desire.

And not any . . . nor any
holy place nor . . .
from which we were absent.

No grove . . . no dance
. . . no sound

Victorian scholars outdid themselves trying to explain this poem as chaste, with one claiming that its subject was nap time at a school for girls. Even more recent interpreters have been reluctant to see it as homoerotic, but an honest reading makes it hard to escape the fact that this poem is about a highly sensual encounter between two female lovers.

The structure of the poem requires three lines for each stanza, so the opening line of the first stanza is missing, and the speaker in the next line is uncertain. Is it Sappho, who is named in the second stanza, or is it the departing lover? While we can't be sure, the better argument is that the speaker is the latter, since the two women in the poem are very different in how they react to their fateful goodbye. The one leaving is distraught, while the other, the poet, takes a more detached tone. A wish for death, even taken as hyperbole, hardly seems to fit with the manner of the Sappho character in the rest of the poem.

"Oh, this has turned out so badly for us, Sappho," cries the unknown woman, but the poet calmly assures her that the memory of their time together will sustain them, particularly one intense encounter heightened by flowers and perfumed myrrh. Roses are an especially powerful symbol of female sexuality in classical poetry, here woven with other flowers on her lover's head, soon followed by garlands on the soft skin of her throat. And just as Hera anoints herself with perfumed oil before seducing Zeus, the unknown lover here anoints herself for Sappho. The climax of the encounter is clear enough for any but the most prudish of interpreters:

> *And on a soft bed*
> *delicate . . .*
> *you let loose your desire.*

The same sixth-century-AD parchment also yielded another fragmentary song by Sappho:

> *. . . Sardis*
> *. . . often turning her thoughts to this*
>
> *. . . you like a goddess*
> *and in your song she delighted most of all.*

Now she stands out among
the women of Lydia,
like the rosy-fingered moon after sunset

surpasses all the stars. Its light
spreads alike over the salty sea
and fields rich in flowers.

The dew is poured forth in beauty,
roses bloom along with tender chevil
and flowering melilot.

She wanders to and fro remembering
gentle Atthis, and her tender
heart is consumed.

Here, Sappho sings of a woman who has gone to the wealthy kingdom of Lydia and its famous capital, Sardis, on the mainland of Asia Minor. This unnamed person misses terribly her beloved, who is not Sappho, but another woman, Atthis. The song would seem fairly straightforward, with Sappho singing of two lovers who are now separated from each other, but it is more complicated than that. Atthis appears in several of Sappho's poems and is mentioned by later commentators as a lover of Sappho. In a line quoted by Hephaestion in his handbook on poetic meters, Sappho sings: "I loved you, Atthis, once long ago." And a badly damaged papyrus from Oxyrhynchus has the simple words "for you, Atthis . . ." The *Suda* encyclopedia names Atthis as one of the companions of Sappho who earned her a bad reputation because of their "shameful friendship."

But however close Sappho and Atthis were at one point, another woman came between them, so that Atthis rejected the poet she once loved. Hephaestion again quotes Sappho:

> *But Atthis, it's become hateful to you to think*
> *of me, and you've flown off to Andromeda.*

Several Sappho fragments mention the poet's bitterness toward her rival, Andromeda, including one brimming with aristocratic distain:

> *What country girl bewitches your mind . . .*
> *dressed in her country clothes . . .*
> *not knowing how to pull her ragged dress over her ankles?*

How, then, does the poem about the unnamed woman who has gone to Lydia and longs for Atthis fit into this picture? It may be that Sappho composed it before she and Atthis were lovers, or that all has been forgiven and Sappho truly sympathizes with Atthis and the woman she has lost. Perhaps the mysterious woman is Andromeda and Sappho sees this parting as an opportunity to win back Atthis with sympathetic words. But in truth, we don't know when Sappho composed this poem, who the departed woman is, or what it tells us about her life. It's much more interesting to look at the words and images we have in this song than to try to fit it into a speculative biography of Sappho.

The most striking feature of this poem is the extended simile. The departed lover stands out among the women of Lydia like the rosy-fingered moon rising among the stars of the night. Sappho's listeners would have immediately recognized the adjective "rosy-fingered" (Greek *rhododaktulos*) as an epithet that Homer used frequently and only with the dawn goddess (Eos). Sappho, as she does so often, turns Homer on his head and makes night into day. Earlier male scholars appreciated the beauty of the simile but saw it as tedious and rambling, full of pointless flowers and dew. Sappho, however, never wastes words.

The Greek goddess of the moon was Selene (*Selanna* in Sappho's Aeolian Greek), sister of the dawn goddess Eos and famed for spreading the nourishing dew across the fields. The goddess of the moon each night bathed in the ocean before mounting her chariot and spreading the life-giving dew across the world—an especially important source of moisture for the earth in the dry summer months. Selene has an ancient pedigree as a goddess sacred to women because of her ties to the female monthly reproductive cycle. One of Sappho's religious poems makes this feminine connection clear:

> *The moon in its fullness appeared,*
> *and when the women took their places around the altar ...*

The choice of flowers watered by the moon is not random either, since roses are, as we saw earlier, a favorite image for the sensuality of the female body. The sexual imagery of dew-covered flowers would have reminded Sappho's listeners once more of the scene in the *Iliad* in which the goddess Hera seduces Zeus in a dew-kissed field of flowers. But here our poet yet again plays her trick of inverting Homer, for a heterosexual tryst of Hera and Zeus becomes a powerful image of longing and love between women in one of Sappho's most beautiful songs.

6

THE GODDESS

In the beginning there was Chaos. Then came into being wide-breasted Gaia—the safe foundation of the deathless ones who hold the peaks of snowy Olympus—and dark Tartarus in the recesses of the wide-pathed earth. And Eros came forth as well, most beautiful of all the immortals, the limb-weakener, who conquers the mind and thoughts of gods and humans alike.

– HESIOD, *THEOGONY*

ANCIENT GREEK RELIGION was very different from most modern Western beliefs. There were hundreds of gods, none of whom were all-knowing or all-powerful. There was no organized "church" of any sort, nor was there a set of beliefs that anyone was required to affirm. The Greeks did not expect their gods to love them or be moral examples for their own lives. There were no creeds, no sacred scriptures, no single path to salvation.

Yet the Greeks were very religious. There were always skeptics and atheists, but the evidence we have suggests that most men and women in ancient times took their worship of the gods quite seriously. It's tempting to see this devotion as a purely business relationship—you give the gods sacrifices and they give you good fortune in return—but such a view can't begin to capture the variety and complexity of Greek religion. Some Greeks performed their sacrifices and went on their way without another thought for the gods, while others devoted their lives to seeking personal salvation and a mystic union with the divine. Just as today, no two people practiced religion in the same way.

In spite of this individuality, religious practice was remarkably similar throughout Greece. The people of Thebes, Sparta, Athens, and Lesbos all worshipped the same gods. There were local variations of religious cults, but no Greek would completely ignore any of the major gods. And just as there was a unity of religion throughout the mainland and islands of Greece, so, too, was there continuity through time. The clay tablets written in the Greek Linear B script that survive from the Bronze Age name many of the same gods who were worshipped by their descendants a thousand years later. This doesn't mean the Greeks weren't open to outside religious influences, especially from the East. Adonis and Cybele from Asia Minor were just two of the many popular divinities imported to Greece. In the polytheistic religion of the ancient Greeks, there was always room for another god.

The gods of Mount Olympus, such as Zeus, Hera, Apollo, and Aphrodite, were worshipped by communities and individuals alike primarily through animal sacrifice. In origin, such sacrifices consisted of a shared sacred meal of gods and humans, with the gods enjoying the sweet savor of the burning fat and entrails while humans feasted on the meat. The sacrifices were not thought of as an atonement for sin, but as a way to honor and gain favor from the gods. Many of these sacrifices were part of public festivals such as those that honored Dionysus or Athena at Athens. Greeks also worshipped different degrees of divine and semidivine beings, ranging from the Olympian gods to wood nymphs and mortal-born heroes. In addition to public opportunities for worship, there were cults restricted to specific groups, such as women, or those of both sexes who had undergone special initiation. The latter category includes the so-called mystery religions—cults so secret that even now we know little about them, except that those who were initiated into them were promised a better fate after death.

As is the case with so many aspects of ancient Greek culture, we know less about the religious life of women than of men. Women were priestesses for the cults of most female divinities, though they could also serve some male gods, such as Dionysus. As we have seen, young girls in Athens were central figures in some community religious rites, and we can be confident this was true throughout Greece. Women were also oracles of the gods, such as the Pythia at Delphi, a woman who sat on a tripod in the temple of Apollo and spoke in verse inspired by the god.

One of the few all-female religious rituals we have any details about is the Thesmophoria festival in which women honored the goddess Demeter. The celebration took place throughout Greece, but wherever it occurred, men were absolutely forbidden to attend. Such single-gender celebrations naturally aroused the discomfort of men accustomed to keeping women in their place. Whether their wives were worshipping Demeter or Dionysus, Greek men often imagined that, once out of firm male control, women would succumb to drunken revelry and unrestrained sexual frenzy. But by all reliable accounts, the religious worship by women was serious and motivated by deep devotion.

Demeter was the goddess of the life-giving earth and the grain that sustained humans and animals alike. She was a child of the Titans Cronus and Rhea, and a sister of Zeus, by whom she had a daughter, Persephone. One day, the maiden Persephone was gathering flowers in a meadow far from home when a giant chasm opened in the ground and out flew Hades, god of the underworld, who seized her and took her against her will to the land of the dead to be his consort. There the young woman wept without ceasing for her mother and the happy life that had been stolen from her. Demeter searched everywhere for Persephone and at last found out that her brother Hades had kidnapped her child. She complained to Zeus but received no help, so she withdrew from Mount Olympus and went into mourning. She wandered the earth as an old mortal woman and became a nursemaid in the home of a local king, taking comfort in caring for the ruler's infant son.

While Demeter was in the king's service, the earth withered from her neglect, and no seed would grow. Famine spread across the world, and people everywhere began to starve. The gods begged Demeter to return, but she refused them. Only when Hades agreed to free Persephone for part of each year did Demeter relent. Thus, the Greeks believed that winter came each year because Persephone returned to Hades and Demeter was once again in mourning. This tale was told by the Greeks to explain the seasons and to remind themselves that they neglected the worship of Demeter at their peril. Zeus might storm and thunder, Poseidon might rule the waves, but it was a goddess who brought life to the world.

For the women of Greece, the Thesmophoria festival in honor of Demeter was an opportunity not only to worship the goddess but to escape the responsibilities of home and husbands for a few days. In Athens, the festival took place in autumn. The first day of the ritual was known as the *anodos*, or "going up," when the women of the city moved in procession to the top of the hill named Pnyx, carrying all they needed for worship, including piglets for sacrifice. On the second day there was fasting and mourning, during which time the women slept on mats woven from plants that reportedly made them lose all interest in sex (as if hunger and sleeping on the ground weren't enough). After this, the piglets were thrown into a deep chasm full of sculpted phalluses and snakes. At the same time, special women known as the Bailers descended into the cave and brought back the decayed remains of the previous year's piglets to place on the altar of Demeter.

As strange as this ritual might seem from the outside, it was a sacred and symbolic descent to the underworld to bring fertility and balance back to the world—and it could be accomplished only by women. A great banquet in honor of the goddess brought the Thesmophoria to an end, after which the weary women descended the hill and returned to their lives as wives and mothers.

. . .

SAPPHO'S POEMS GIVE us haunting, tantalizing, extraordinary images of the religious life of women. There is nothing in them like the grand Thesmophoria—though such a festival was probably practiced on Lesbos—but instead something more deeply personal and profoundly moving.

Consider again the first poem in Sappho's collection, in which she calls on the goddess Aphrodite for help to win the heart of another woman:

Deathless Aphrodite on your dazzling throne,
child of Zeus, weaver of snares, I pray to you,
do not, with anguish and pain, O Lady,
    break my heart.

But come here now, if ever in the past,
listening, you heard my cries from afar
and leaving your father's golden house,
    you came to me,

yoking your chariot. Beautiful swift sparrows
drew you over the black earth
with their whirling wings, down from the sky
    through the middle of the air,

and quickly they arrived. And you, O Blessed Goddess,
with a smile on your immortal face,

*asked what was the matter now and why
had I called you again*

*and what I wanted most of all to happen,
me, with my crazy heart: "Who should I persuade this time
to lead you back to her love? Who is it, Sappho,
who has done you wrong?*

*For even if she runs away, soon she will pursue.
If she refuses gifts, she'll be giving instead.
And if she won't love, she will soon enough,
even against her will."*

*So come to me now, free me from unbearable
pain. All my heart yearns to happen—
make it happen. You yourself,
be my ally.*

The song begins as a formal and reverent prayer of petition to Aphrodite, but it quickly becomes an intimate conversation between Sappho and the goddess. Aphrodite hears the cry of a woman in pain and leaves the heights of Olympus to come to her. With a smile on her face, Aphrodite speaks to Sappho as an old friend: "Who should I persuade *this* time to lead you back to her love?" This is not the normal tone used by Greek gods when addressing mortals. Homer's heroes rightly quake with fear when Zeus or Poseidon speak to them. Only Odysseus in his dealings with the goddess Athena comes anywhere close to this level of intimacy. Sappho's Aphrodite is, as the last line of the poem says, her *summachos* ("ally")—a word of war frequently used in Homer by equals who stand together in battle.

Sappho also employs images of closeness between herself and Aphrodite elsewhere in her poems:

I talked with you in a dream, Cyprus-born

And Aphrodite addresses Sappho in another fragment:

. . . you and my servant Love

This degree of intimacy between mortal and divine in ancient Greek literature isn't unique to Sappho, but it is unusual and begs the question of whether these poems reflect an aspect of the religious life of women not attested to in the descriptions by men. Are we witnessing here a spiritual relationship between women and goddesses that was largely alien to a male world, or are these invocations and imagined conversations with the divine simply poetic devices that have no bearing on the religious lives of real women? It's impossible to know for certain, but other poems by Sappho suggest there was an unappreciated depth in the spiritual lives of Greek women.

ONE OF THE oldest preserved poems of Sappho comes from an *ostrakon*, or potsherd, a broken piece of pottery used in ancient times for informal writing such as tax receipts, military orders, and school exercises. This particular piece contains four stanzas of a poem by Sappho recorded in Egypt in the third century BC and now preserved in the Laurentian Library in Florence, Italy. The writing is not always clear, and several words are missing, but what survives is once again a remarkable prayer of invocation addressed to the goddess Aphrodite:

> *Come to me here from Crete to this holy*
> *temple, to your delightful grove of apple*
> *trees, where altars smoke*
>   *with frankincense.*
>
> *Here cold water babbles through apple*
> *branches, roses shadow all,*
> *and from quivering leaves*
>   *a deep sleep falls.*
>
> *Here too is a meadow for grazing horses*
> *blossoming with spring flowers and breezes*
> *blowing sweet like honey . . .*
>
> *In this place you . . . taking, O Cypris,*
> *gracefully into golden cups*
> *nectar mingled with our festivities*
>   *pour now.*

Scholars can't agree whether this is an imagined scene or an actual hymn used in worship, but in either case it's a song of powerful religious imagery evoking a mystical union of worshippers, the goddess, and the natural setting of her outdoor temple.

Sappho weaves a profoundly sensual prayer with her use of sight, smell, taste, and sound in the lush and primal grove of Aphrodite. Apples, a symbol of love and a fruit of the autumn, mingle with roses and other flowers of the spring in a magical place removed from time. The worshippers hear the babbling water of a sacred spring echoing through the branches above and see the dappled shadows of blossoming roses, a powerful image of female sexuality favored elsewhere by Sappho. They can smell sweet frankincense burning on the altar, feel the gentle, warm wind from the meadow on their skin, and taste the nectar, a food of the gods, poured into golden cups for their festivities by the goddess herself. From above through the quivering leaves, a deep sleep falls down upon them—and not just any sleep. It is a *koma*, or hypnotic sleep, of enchantment, a powerful trance such as that which descends on Zeus after making love with Hera or which overcomes an audience listening to a skilled bard sing and play the lyre.

This gathering of women worshippers is echoed in another poem of Sappho mentioned in Chapter 5:

> *The moon in its fullness appeared,*
> *and when the women took their places around the altar . . .*

This fragment is another rare glimpse into the private religious life of women in ancient Greece. The moon, as seen earlier, is a

Libation bowl with young women dancing around
an altar (c. 450 BC).

(MUSEUM OF FINE ARTS, BOSTON)

powerful feminine symbol that oversees the worshippers as they
gather around the altar at night. Whether this is a sacrifice to
Aphrodite or another goddess is unknown, but the solemnity of

the occasion is clear even from only two lines. We don't know whether Sappho was a priestess or leader of a religious cult herself, but these two poems do speak of her as a participant in worship in a time and place set apart by women for themselves.

IN ANOTHER FRAGMENTARY poem, Sappho invokes Hera, the wife of Zeus and a goddess favorable to women in all phases of their lives:

> *Come close to me, I pray,*
> *Lady Hera, and may your graceful form appear,*
> *you to whom the sons of Atreus prayed,*
> *those glorious kings,*
>
> *after they had accomplished many great deeds,*
> *first at Troy, then on the sea.*
> *They came to this island, but they could not*
> *complete their voyage home*
>
> *until they called on you and Zeus the god of suppliants*
> *and Thyone's lovely child.*
> *So now be kind and help me too,*
> *as in ancient days.*
>
> *Holy and beautiful . . .*
> *virgin . . .*
> *around . . .*

to be . . .
to arrive . . .

It's possible this is a choral song sung by a group of women wor-shipping Hera, or it could be a private prayer by Sappho, perhaps for the safe return of a loved one from a sea voyage, as we've seen elsewhere. We know that the sons of Atreus she refers to in the first stanza are Agamemnon and Menelaus. In Homer's version of the story, Agamemnon stays at Troy after the war to appease the angry goddess Athena, but his brother Menelaus, along with aged Nestor and Odysseus, sails away. Odysseus soon returns to Agamemnon, but Nestor and presumably Menelaus continue to nearby Lesbos to seek a sign from Zeus about the best route for the voyage home. Here Sappho is presenting an alternate local tradition in which both brothers arrive together in Lesbos to pray to the trio of Zeus, Hera, and Dionysus, Thyone's love child, and a god particularly worshipped by women.

Sappho's contemporary Alcaeus also sings of this peculiarly Lesbian trinity:

> *The people of Lesbos founded*
> *a great and conspicuous temple precinct*
> *to be held by all and placed in it*
> *altars of the blessed immortals.*
> *They named there Zeus, god of suppliants,*
> *and you, Hera, the glorious goddess of Aeolia,*
> *mother of all, and third Kemelios, Dionysus,*
> *eater of raw flesh . . .*

Alcaeus and a later ancient commentator also say that the section of the temple devoted to Hera was the site of an annual beauty contest for the women of Lesbos, who gave a sacred shout each year in honor of the goddess.

In this poem Sappho once again turns Homer on his head by deliberately presenting a different tradition and adding the goddess Hera along with Dionysus as a trio of gods the brothers once prayed to. Then she herself sets aside the two male gods and invokes Hera alone, both building on and altering the legendary precedent laid down by the sons of Atreus in Homer's tale.

A FINAL FRAGMENT of a religious poem composed by Sappho and quoted by Hephaestion once again addresses Aphrodite. It is our earliest evidence of the imported Eastern cult of Adonis:

> *"Delicate Adonis is dying, Cytherea—what should we*
> *do?"*
> *"Beat your breasts, girls, and tear your clothes."*

This song is a different sort from the previous poems. We have here part of a group ritual in which women call on Aphrodite (Cytherea) in mourning for the handsome young Adonis.

Adonis was a mortal born from an incestuous affair who attracted the attention of Aphrodite. She entrusted him to the underworld goddess Persephone, who also fell in love with the boy and refused to give him back. In judgment, Zeus decreed that Adonis would spend four months each year in Hades with

Persephone, four months with Aphrodite, and the other four months with whomever he chose. He picked Aphrodite and enjoyed his life with her until he died in a hunting accident in the arms of his heartbroken lover.

Each year, Adonis was mourned by the women of Greece as an emblem of the fragility of life. To honor him in Athens, women planted seeds in broken pots in the midsummer heat so that they soon withered and died. The Athenian celebration was a noisy, obscene, and public affair of women that alternated between joy and grief. A similar religious celebration almost certainly happened annually on Lesbos. And although we may long to know more, the images we do have in Sappho's poetry provide us with a unique, inside glimpse into the religious life of women in ancient Greece.

7

UNYIELDING TIME

*It's not by strength or swiftness or dexterity that great things are
achieved, but by reflection, character, and judgment. In these respects
old age is not poorer but richer.*

– CICERO, *ON GROWING OLD*

WOMEN IN THE ancient world were lucky to live past the age of forty. Given the ravages of disease, the backbreaking work of farm and domestic life, and the dangers of frequent childbirth, most wives and mothers could only dream of attaining the biblical three score and ten years. A Roman gravestone from North Africa records a typical story: "Here lies Ennia Fructosa, dearest wife, whose modesty was evident and obedience praised. She was married at age fifteen and accepted the title of wife. She lived no more than thirteen years after her wedding."

But there were exceptions. Elderly women from the poorest families who had given birth to many children could be seen gathered around every village well, trading gossip. By fate or natural disposition, they had beaten the odds to reach sixty, seventy, or beyond. In an age when women of succeeding generations gave birth to their first child soon after puberty, it was possible to find five generations of girls and matrons living together in a single household. For a woman like Sappho from a wealthy family with slaves to perform the harshest tasks and access to the best medicine of the day, the odds of long life were even better.

As with most aspects of women's lives in the ancient world, we know precious little about how they themselves viewed growing older. Men were little help. The Roman orator Cicero composed an entire book on the joys and sorrows of aging without once mentioning what the experience was like for a woman.

The Greeks had no concept of middle age. Men passed from being *neoi* (young adults) to *presbyteroi* (elders) with nothing in between. On those rare occasions when a man is called *mesos*, or "middle-aged," in Greek literature, it's usually a term of derision for those who can't come to terms with growing older, as in a story by the second-century-AD Greek writer Babrius:

> *There was once a man of middle age who was neither*
> *young nor old but had white and black hairs mixed*
> *together on his head. Yet still he spent his time carousing*
> *with women. He was sleeping with two women, one who*
> *was young and the other older. The young woman wanted*
> *him to look like a lover her own age, so she plucked out*
> *his white hairs. The woman in her prime wanted him*
> *to look more mature, so she plucked out his black hairs.*
> *Eventually the two women left the man bald.*

Adult women were divided into those of childbearing years and those beyond menopause. A wife who bore her husband sons and lived beyond the time when she could bear children was honored and achieved a degree of freedom unknown to younger women. Such a respected matron was free to go outside her home by herself, since she was no longer at risk of becoming pregnant by another man. As the fourth-century-BC Athenian orator Hyperides said: "A woman who leaves her house ought to have reached that stage of life when those who see her don't ask whose wife she is but whose mother she is." Greek medical writers, such as Aristotle, agreed that most women reached menopause in their forties. These male commentators were also quick to point out that women going through this change of life could be emotional and unpredictable.

For women who survived into their forties and beyond, life could be very pleasant. Most would have been married in their teens to men almost a generation older than themselves, so that by the time they passed menopause their husbands would often have died from old age. However much they loved their spouses, these women for the first time in their lives were free to make choices for themselves.

The financial support of widowed matrons fell to their sons, who generally treated them with great respect and affection. To ill-treat or ignore his mother brought great shame on a man. A woman without sons faced a more problematic future. Her relatives, daughters, or late husband's extended family would usually provide for her, but sometimes elderly matrons struggled to eke out a living by serving as midwives or as professional mourners at funerals. Older female slaves could be cherished and valuable members of a household, as was the aged nurse Eurycleia in the home of Odysseus, but there must have been many who were left to starve when they became too sick or feeble to serve their masters any longer.

GREEKS FEARED THE process of dying more than death itself. For most, life after death was a vague and uncertain concept. Even if they believed in an afterlife, it wasn't necessarily something they looked forward to. This attitude led to an appreciation for living, especially among older people. When the mythical king Admetus hears that he is doomed to death unless he can find someone to take his place, he asks his aged parents to die for him, but his father refuses, even though he is old, saying: "It is precious, this light the gods send, yes precious."

The earliest literary portrayal of life after death is the dismal Hades of Homer, to which almost everyone went, regardless of their actions in life. When the living Odysseus visits the shade of Achilles in Hades and praises him for being famous in the afterlife, the hero of Troy rebukes him:

> *O shining Odysseus, don't try to console me for dying. I would rather follow the plow as the slave of a landless farmer struggling to survive than be king over all the dead.*

Homer's dead spent eternity wandering the twilight realm of Hades unable to speak unless some rare visitor gave them blood to drink. As Sappho herself says to a woman she disliked:

> *But when you die you will lie there and there will be no*
>   *memory*
> *of you nor longing for you after, for you have no share in*
>   *the roses*
> *of Pieria. But you will wander unseen in the house of*
>   *Hades,*
> *flying about among the shadowy dead.*

It was not a fate to be envied, but neither was it feared by most. There were, however, those who hoped for something more, whether philosophers or followers of mystery religions. For these there was the possibility of a pleasant afterlife or reincarnation here on earth.

WHATEVER A GREEK'S attitude about life after death, the proper care of the dead was of the greatest importance—and it was a ritual presided over largely by women. The first stage was the preparation of the body at home, starting with the closing of the mouth and eyes by the next of kin. It was the shutting of the eyes that allowed the *psyche*, or soul, to leave the body.

The women of the house would next bathe the body with seawater, if available, and then anoint and dress the deceased in a long robe or wrap the body in a shroud of white linen cloth. The corpse was then placed on a wooden bed with the feet pointing toward the door. A virgin who had died would be dressed as a bride, while soldiers were often attired in their uniforms. Jewelry was common for the deceased, depending on the means of the family. Funerals in Sappho's time could be particularly extravagant, prompting some cities to pass laws against ostentatious displays aimed at impressing the neighbors. Funeral rites required no fixed service or particular words, but images of ritual mourning by women frequently appear on Greek vases. The women would tear at their hair, beat their breasts, and sing songs of lamentation, while the men stood by in quiet grief.

After a respectful time of mourning, the body was taken from the house before sunrise and carried on a bier or transported in a wagon to the site of deposition. Men with weapons led the way, while the women followed behind. A wealthy family might hire musicians to accompany the procession. Families had plots outside the precincts of the town, where the body was either burned or placed in a coffin and buried. With cremation, the fires of ancient times were not usually hot enough to completely burn the bones. These were collected and placed in jars after the ashes had cooled. Priests were not present and, in fact, were forbidden to attend burials, lest they be ritually polluted by the closeness of death. In early Greek times, sacrifices were performed for the dead, perhaps by the women of the household.

After the interment of the remains, men and women left the cemetery separately. It's likely that the men stayed behind to close the grave and seal the tomb, while the women returned home and prepared a meal for all the family gathered to honor the dead.

As with the rest of Sappho's life, we have only glimpses of her later years. We can presume she returned home from exile in Sicily at some point in the early sixth century BC and again took up her life on Lesbos as a poet. We know that her daughter, Cleis, was with her as she grew older, and since she never mentions any sons, it's likely that Sappho lived with Cleis. We know nothing of Sappho's relationships with other women in her later years, nor do we know whether the friends who had once gathered around her to hear her songs were still part of her life. But we do know something about how Sappho viewed growing older, thanks to a remarkable poem rediscovered in a two-part story over the last century.

In 1922 there was great excitement among the small community of papyrologists when a new fragment of one of Sappho's poems was published after being discovered in the familiar trash heaps of Oxyrhynchus. Unfortunately, the papyrus was in even worse shape than most, with only a handful of legible words:

> . . . *beautiful gifts . . . children*
> . . . *the sweet-sounding lyre dear to song*
> . . . *old age . . . my skin now*
> . . . *hair once black*
> . . . *knees do not carry*
> . . . *like fawns*

. . . but what can be done?

. . . not possible to become

. . . rosey-armed Dawn

. . . carrying to the ends of the earth.

. . . yet seized . . . wife

The poem clearly showed Sappho writing about growing older, but what was she trying to say? The words were her typical blend of stark reality and beautiful imagery with a possible reference at the end to a well-known myth about the goddess of the dawn carrying off the handsome mortal Tithonus in a futile attempt to make him her immortal lover. But with so little of the poem surviving, there was not much more to say. It was given the catalog number 58 in the Sappho corpus, published in a collection of papyri excavated that year, and soon forgotten by all but a few Greek scholars.

Then, exactly eighty years later, something remarkable happened. An antiquities dealer in Europe let it be known that he had in his possession a small collection of papyrus fragments from Egypt. Where exactly these came from and how he had acquired them were a mystery, but a quick inspection confirmed they were genuine. To save these treasures, the University of Cologne in Germany purchased them for its archives. And only a short time later, two researchers, Michael Gronewald and Robert Daniel, working with one of these fragments from the wrappings of a mummy, announced in a scholarly journal that they had found some of the missing pieces of Sappho 58. With this discovery, a still fragmentary but much more complete poem could be read for the first time in two thousand years:

> . . . *beautiful gifts of the violet-laden Muses, children*
> . . . *the sweet-sounding lyre dear to song.*
> . . . *my skin once soft is wrinkled now,*
> . . . *my hair once black has turned to white.*
> *My heart has become heavy, my knees*
> *that once danced nimbly like fawns cannot carry me.*
> *How often I lament these things—but what can be done?*
> *No one who is human can escape old age.*
> *They say that Dawn with arms like roses once took*
> *Tithonus, beautiful and young, carrying him to the*
> *ends of the earth. But in time grey old age still*
> *found him, even though he had an immortal wife.*

This discovery was so startling that the *Times Literary Supplement* soon published an article describing the find and included the original Greek text along with an English translation. Newspapers and media outlets around the world picked up the story, so that in a matter of days millions of people were reading the new Sappho poem translated into Afrikaans, Chinese, Spanish, and Urdu.

But regardless of the language in which the poem was published, the talent of its creator was clear. The visual and physical images she creates of aging show that the older Sappho had lost none of the skill that created the moving songs of love she had composed in her youth. Readers can see and feel the aging process that has overtaken her. Those of a certain age can identify with the unfamiliar face in the mirror and pain in the knees on cold mornings. Memories of youthful dances return, as distant now as a light heart and supple limbs.

But, ever realistic, Sappho asks, What can a person do? Growing older is simply part of being human. To fight against time is both foolish and futile. The goddess of the dawn learned this when she fell in love with the young and handsome prince Tithonus and obtained immortality for him from Zeus—but she foolishly forgot to ask for eternal youth as well. And so, as the years went by, her lover shriveled into a creature with only a shrill voice remaining who eventually turned into a cicada.

The Greek scholar M. L. West summed up the reaction of many to the new poem when he called it "a small masterpiece, simple, concise, perfectly formed, an honest, unpretentious expression of feeling, dignified in its restraint." Others could only borrow the words of the poet Algernon Charles Swinburne: "Sappho is simply nothing less . . . than the greatest poet who ever was."

WE DON'T KNOW how long Sappho lived after composing her poem on growing older, but it's likely she died an old woman. One final poem gives us a hint at how she faced death. Maximus of Tyre, in his *Orations*, quotes these two lines after saying that just as Socrates chastised his companions for weeping as he drank the hemlock cup, Sappho was angry at her daughter Cleis as she cried for her mother at the end and chastised her:

> *It is not right in the house of those serving the Muses*
> *for there to be lamenting. That would not be fitting for us.*

The gift of poetry was Sappho's comfort in her final days. To complain to the gods about life coming to an end would have been ungrateful for one who had been so blessed. Whatever she believed awaited her after death, Sappho knew her songs would live on.

EPILOGUE

Someone, I say, will remember us in time to come.

– SAPPHO, POEM 147

OUR PORTRAIT OF Sappho—who she was, what her life was like, and how she was able to overcome such enormous obstacles in a male-dominated world to become one of the greatest poets of all time—is woefully incomplete. In the end we find ourselves longing for so much more than the scattered fragments of her poetry can tell us. We can only hope that more of her poems will be discovered in the future that will help us understand this remarkable woman—but for now we are left wanting.

Sappho was certainly the first and greatest of the women poets in the ancient world, but she was not the only one. We know of about a hundred such women, though their works also survive mostly in fragments. All of these women would have known Sappho's works, and many were clearly inspired by her example.

One of the earliest was Myrtis from Boeotia north of Athens, a lyric poet of perhaps the late sixth century BC who was reportedly the teacher of the famous poet Pindar. None of Myrtis's songs survive, but we do have a paraphrase in the later Greek author Plutarch, who says she composed a poem about a woman named Ochna who falsely accused a man of rape after he rejected her love. Ochna's brothers in righteous anger slew the man, but she confessed her lie to save her brothers from death and subsequently threw herself off a cliff. As much as this sounds like a condemnation of Ochna and the deceitfulness of women in general, it's quite possible that Myrtis was more nuanced in her tale than Plutarch reveals.

In the next century, a woman named Corinna from the same region of Greece as Myrtis composed lyric poetry that filled five books. She was reportedly a rival of Pindar and beat him five times in poetry contests. Corinna's works survive, like Sappho's, mostly in papyrus fragments discovered in modern times. As for her subjects, as Corinna herself says:

> *I sing of the great deeds*
> *of heroes, men and women alike.*

From the scraps of her songs that survive, Corinna's poems seem to have been based largely on local myths and legends, such as a singing contest between two mountains in which they tell the story of the goddess Rhea saving her baby Zeus from being devoured by his father, Cronos. In another fragment she sings of how the nine daughters of the local river god were taken and raped by Zeus and other male deities, but counsels their father to console himself that they will be immortal and the mothers of demigods.

Praxilla of Sicyon near Corinth was a popular fifth-century-BC poet who composed hymns, choral lyrics, and drinking songs. Only a few of her fragments survive, but they show a sharp and wicked sense of humor. To those who would be unduly optimistic about life, she warns:

> *O friend, watch out for a scorpion under every stone.*

And speaking to a member of her own gender:

> *O you who gaze in such beauty from your window,*
> *a virgin from the neck up but an experienced woman*
> *below.*

In the same century as Praxilla lived Telesilla of Argos to the south, a woman known long after for her poetry but even more so for her military abilities. When Argos was attacked by the Spartans while the men were away, Telesilla gave the women of the town weapons and led them to the city walls. They all fought bravely and held the enemy off until the men of Sparta gave up out of shame at being defeated by women. The people of Argos later built a statue in her honor.

The woman with the best claim of being second only to Sappho in poetic skill is the fourth-century-BC writer Erinna, whose brief but moving poem *The Distaff* lamenting the death of her childhood friend Baucis we encountered in Chapter 1. Composed in the same hexameter meter as Homer's epics, *The Distaff* was considered a short masterpiece in ancient times. Only a little over fifty of the original three hundred lines survive, rediscovered on papyrus in the twentieth century. One ancient writer was so impressed with Erinna's poem that he gave her the highest compliment by comparing her to both Homer and Sappho:

> *This is the Lesbian honeycomb of Erinna.*
>> *Even though it is small, it is flavored with*
>> *the honey of the Muses.*
> *Her three-hundred lines are equal to Homer,*
>> *though she was only a girl of nineteen.*
> *She worked the distaff out of fear of her mother,*
>> *and at the loom she stood as a servant*
>> *of the Muses.*
> *Sappho is better than Erinna at lyric poetry*
>> *by as much as Erinna is better than Sappho at*
>> *hexameters.*

Soon after Erinna, the Hellenistic period began, in which there were several female Greek poets whose fame lasted for centuries. Anyte from the Arcadian mountains of southern Greece lived about 300 BC and wrote beautiful epigrams, often with a pastoral background inspired by the countryside of her homeland. About twenty of these poems survive, all of them short verses of consummate skill set in the form of inscriptions on tombstones. Four are dedicated to young women, including:

No bedchamber and sacred marriage rites for you.
> *Instead your mother has placed upon this marble*
>> *tomb*
a likeness of your girlish shape and beauty,
> *Thersis, so I can speak to you though you are dead.*

Anyte also wrote more playful epigrams for animals such as horses, dogs, birds, dolphins, and even insects:

For her grasshopper, nightingale of the fields,
> *and her cicada, dweller in the oak, Myro made a*
>> *common tomb.*
The girls shed a virgin's tears, since Hades, hard to
> *persuade,*
>> *twice came and took away her playmates.*

A contemporary of Anyte was Nossis, a woman who lived in the Greek town of Locri in southern Italy. The town was unusual, according to the Greek historian Polybius, for having a ruling aristocracy based on descent from mothers rather than the normal paternal lineage. Nossis was clearly a great admirer of Sappho and echoes Sappho's themes in her poems:

Nothing is sweeter than Eros. All other delights are
> *second to Love. Even honey I spit from my mouth.*
Nossis proclaims this: Whoever Aphrodite has not loved
> *doesn't know what sort of blossoms her roses are.*

In another epigram, Nossis names Sappho and continues her predecessor's image of flowers as a symbol of female sexuality:

> *Stranger, if you sail to Mytilene of the beautiful dances,*
> > *to be inspired by the flower of Sappho's charms,*
> *say that the land of Locri bore one dear to the Muses,*
> > *and when you have learned my name is Nossis,*
> > *then depart.*

Nossis's other poems are also portraits of women, including a professional prostitute:

> *Come to the temple and let us gaze on the image of*
> > *Aphrodite,*
> > *made with a trim of gold.*
> *Polyarchis dedicated it, after earning great wealth*
> > *gained from her own splendid body.*

The Hellenistic period yielded to the age of Rome, in which a few educated women took up their pens to write poems in Latin, though always under the influence of Sappho's Greek verses. The best known of these is Sulpicia, who lived during the reign of the emperor Augustus. Sulpicia's six surviving poems celebrate a passionate love affair she had with a man before her marriage—a daring blow for women's sexual independence during the strict moral climate of Augustus's rule:

At last love has come—and the rumor that I've covered it up
    would cause me more shame than to lay it bare for
        all to see.
Begged by my Muses, Cytherea has lifted him up
    and put him in my lap.
Venus has kept her promises. If there's anyone with no joys
    of their own, let them tell of mine.
I would not entrust my words to sealed tablets,
    lest someone read them before my beloved.
I am delighted to have gone astray. It bores me to keep up
    appearances.
      Let them say that I, a worthy woman, have been
        with a worthy man.

THE ANCIENT GREEK verb for performing oral sex on a man was *lesbiazein*—a distinctly heterosexual term derived from the women of Lesbos who were rumored to have unquenchable lust for members of the opposite sex. There was no surer way to get a laugh from an audience at a comedy performance in fourth-century-BC Athens than to include a female character from Lesbos—played by a man, of course, as in Shakespeare's day—lurching across the stage in search of her latest male conquest. And of all the women of Lesbos, none played to the crowd better than Sappho.

How a woman so clearly devoted in her poetry to love for

other women became a stock figure of same-sex lust and at the same time one of the most admired authors from ancient times to the modern day is a testimony to the power of each generation to re-create historical figures to fit their own desires. The legacy of Sappho for over two thousand years has been that of inspired genius, prostitute, prim schoolmistress, feminist icon, or any number of other roles, depending on whom you read.

The Greek philosopher Plato was an admirer of Sappho, calling her *sophe* ("wise") and reportedly observing:

> *Some people say there are nine Muses—how foolish!*
> *See here now, Sappho of Lesbos is the tenth.*

But not all of Plato's contemporaries were so respectful. A favorite theme in comic plays had Sappho falling madly in love with a mythical ferryman named Phaon, swearing off of women forever, and then throwing herself off a cliff when Phaon rejected her advances. As the writer Menander says:

> *Sappho, so goes the story,*
> > *in crazed love pursued the proud Phaon*
> *and leapt from a far-seen promontory.*

But throughout classical times, most took Sappho more seriously. The Romans were great readers of Greek poetry, and since any educated Roman knew Greek, Sappho greatly influenced the best of Latin verse. If imitation is the greatest form of tribute, the

Roman poet Catullus in the first century BC shows himself one of the leading admirers of Sappho. Generations of Latin students have studied his Poem 51:

> *That man seems to me equal to a god,*
> *that man, if it's right to say so, surpasses the gods,*
> *who sitting opposite you,*
>   *looks at you and listens*
>
> *to your sweet laughter. This rips away*
> *my senses, for as soon as I look at you,*
> *Lesbia, no voice remains*
>   *in my mouth,*
>
> *my tongue is paralyzed, a subtle flame*
> *runs down my limbs, my ears ring*
> *with their own sound, and my eyes*
>   *are veiled in darkness.*

Catullus keeps much of the language and style of Sappho's original poem, even rendering his version in the same poetic meter, but the most striking alteration he makes is to change its homoerotic tone to the passionate love of a man for a woman, his mistress Lesbia.

Other leading Roman poets were equally reverential, including Horace and Ovid. Horace praises Sappho, along with Homer, Pindar, and others, as the greatest of Greek poets:

. . . the love
of the Aeolian girl breathes still, and with this key
her passions still faithfully live.

In the Days of Sappho, by John William Godward (1904).
(J. PAUL GETTY MUSEUM)

Ovid, who was banished to the coast of the Black Sea by Augustus for his erotic poetry, wrote back to a young woman poet in Rome that, with effort, she could be second only to Sappho:

So if the fire still burns in your breast as before
only the woman from Lesbos will surpass you.

But Ovid was also responsible for popularizing the myth of Sappho and the ferryman Phaon. So great was his influence in western Europe that from the Middle Ages into modern times, the little anyone knew of her was as a lovesick, suicidal woman unable to win the heart of the man she so desperately desired.

In time, the Roman Empire passed away and Christianity rose to replace the ancient gods. Knowledge of the Greek language faded in the West and, with it, those who could appreciate Sappho in her original tongue. Only in the Byzantine Empire did a few continue to read the remaining copies of Sappho's poems. Eustathius, a deacon at the grand church of Saint Sophia in Constantinople and later a saint, was perhaps the last Greek scholar who had access to the whole of Sappho's writings. He lectured on ancient Greek literature, including Sappho, and preserved a few lines of her poetry in his commentary on Homer's *Iliad*:

The stars around the beautiful moon
hide back their radiant form
when she in her fullness shines
over the earth.

These are the final words of Sappho from the ancient world. Even scholars from the same century as Eustathius no longer knew her works. As the Byzantine writer Tzetzes says: "The passage of time has destroyed Sappho and her poems, her lyre and her songs."

Not until the sixteenth and seventeenth centuries did scholars begin to translate Sappho's songs into the modern languages of Europe. French, German, and English editions of her works began to appear, pieced together from the scattered fragments preserved in obscure Greek grammatical tracts, so that by Victorian times the poet of Lesbos had again become a major literary figure. The discovery of almost a hundred papyrus fragments of Sappho's poems over the last century has increased her reputation even more. With each new find, readers can marvel at the genius of a poet whose words are as fresh and vibrant today as they were more than two thousand years ago.

THE POEMS OF SAPPHO

T HE FOLLOWING IS a translation of all of Sappho's surviv-
ing poetry for readers to enjoy. In a few cases we are fortu-
nate to have a complete or almost complete poem, though this is
the exception rather than the rule. More often we have a single
stanza, part of a line, or even just a single word. Yet even a word
by itself can have beauty.

My translation and numbering of the poems is based on the
Greek text of *Sappho et Alcaeus: Fragmenta* (Amsterdam: Ath-
enaeum, 1971), edited by Eva-Maria Voigt. I used other schol-
arly editions as well, including Edgar Lobel and Denys Page's
Poetarum Lesbiorum Fragmenta (Oxford: Clarendon, 1968) and
David A. Campbell's *Greek Lyric I: Sappho and Alcaeus* (Cam-
bridge, MA: Harvard University Press, 2002). In many cases
I was able to refer to high-quality photographs of the papyrus
fragments themselves. In one instance, I was able to hold the
only surviving copy of a Sappho poem (44) in my hands at the
papyrology rooms of the Sackler Library at Oxford University.
Next to the birth of my children, it was one of the most thrilling
moments of my life.

The sources for each poem, along with occasional brief com-

mentary, are given in the notes. In the poems that survive in
fragments, ellipses (. . .) indicate gaps in the lines. In many cases,
whole lines are missing between the gaps.

No translation of an ancient Greek author can do justice to
the original, especially when that author is a poet as subtle as
Sappho. In rendering her beautiful songs into English, I strug-
gled with the often-competing goals of accuracy and readability.
But as much as possible in all the poems, I tried to let Sappho
speak to us through the centuries with her own voice.

1.

Deathless Aphrodite on your dazzling throne,
child of Zeus, weaver of snares, I pray to you,
do not, with anguish and pain, O Lady,
   break my heart.

But come here now, if ever in the past,
listening, you heard my cries from afar
and leaving your father's golden house,
   you came to me,

yoking your chariot. Beautiful swift sparrows
drew you over the black earth
with their whirling wings, down from the sky
   through the middle of the air,

and quickly they arrived. And you, O Blessed Goddess,
with a smile on your immortal face,
asked what was the matter now and why
        had I called you again

and what I wanted most of all to happen,
me, with my crazy heart: "Who should I persuade this time
to lead you back to her love? Who is it, Sappho,
        who has done you wrong?

For even if she runs away, soon she will pursue.
If she refuses gifts, she'll be giving instead.
And if she won't love, she will soon enough,
        even against her will."

So come to me now, free me from unbearable
pain. All my heart yearns to happen—
make it happen. You yourself,
        be my ally.

2.

Come to me here from Crete to this holy
temple, to your delightful grove of apple
trees, where altars smoke
        with frankincense.

Here cold water babbles through apple
branches, roses shadow all,
and from quivering leaves
                    a deep sleep falls.

Here too is a meadow for grazing horses
blossoming with spring flowers and breezes
blowing sweet like honey . . .

In this place you . . . taking, O Cypris,
gracefully into golden cups
nectar mingled with our festivities
                    pour now.

3.

. . . to give
. . . yet of the glorious
. . . of the beautiful and good
. . . pain
. . . blame
. . . swollen
. . . you have your fill, for
. . . not so
. . . is settled
. . . nor
. . . I understand

. . . of wickedness

. . . other

. . . minds

. . . blessed

4.

. . . heart

. . . completely

. . . I can

. . . would be for me

. . . to shine back

. . . face

. . . joined together

5.

. . . Nereids, grant that
my brother come back to me unharmed
and that all he wishes for in his heart
comes true.

And grant that he atone for all his past mistakes.
Make him a joy to his friends and a grief
to his enemies. And may no one bring us sorrow
ever again.

May he wish to bring honor
to his sister, but dismal grief . . .
. . . sorrowing before
. . . listening, millet seed
. . . of the citizens
. . . not again
. . . but you, Cypris
. . . putting aside evil

6.

Go . . .
so that we may see . . .
Lady . . .
of golden arms . . .
fate . . .

7.

of Doricha . . .
commands, for not . . .
arrogance . . .
for young men . . .
beloved . . .

8.

for you, Atthis...

9.

invites...
all not...
a feast...
for Hera...

12.

...thought
...barefoot

15.

...blessed

...that he atone for his past mistakes
...with fortune of the harbor
...Cypris, and may she find you very harsh.
And may she—that Doricha—not boast, saying
he came a second time

        to her longed-for love.

16.

Some say an army of horsemen, others a host of infantry,
others a fleet of ships is the most beautiful thing
on the black earth. But I say
                    it's whatever you love.

It's perfectly easy to make this clear
to everyone. For she who surpassed
all in beauty—Helen—left behind
                    her most noble husband

and went sailing off to Troy,
giving no thought at all to her child
or dear parents, but . . .
                    led her astray.

. . . for
. . . lightly
. . . reminded me now of Anactoria
                    who is not here.

I would rather see her lovely walk
and her bright sparkling face
than the chariots of the Lydians
                    or infantry in arms.

. . . not possible to happen

. . . to pray to share
. . . unexpected

17.

Come close to me, I pray,
Lady Hera, and may your graceful form appear,
you to whom the sons of Atreus prayed,
            those glorious kings,

after they had accomplished many great deeds,
first at Troy, then on the sea.
They came to this island, but they could not
            complete their voyage home

until they called on you and Zeus the god of suppliants
and Thyone's lovely child.
So now be kind and help me too,
            as in ancient days.

Holy and beautiful . . .
virgin . . .
around . . .

to be . . .
to arrive . . .

18.

all . . .
to say . . .
my tongue . . .
to tell stories . . .
for a man . . .
greater . . .

19.

. . . waiting
. . . in sacrifices
. . . having good
. . . but going
. . . for we know
. . . of works
. . . after
. . . and toward
. . . says this

20.

. . . brightness and
. . . with good fortune
. . . to reach the harbor

. . . *black earth*

. . . *sailors*

. . . *great gusts of wind*

. . . *on dry land*

. . . *sail*

. . . *the cargo*

. . . *since*

. . . *many*

. . . *tasks*

. . . *dry land*

21.

. . . *pity*

. . . *trembling*

. . . *my skin, old age now*

. . . *covers*

. . . *flies pursuing*

. . . *noble*

. . . *taking*

. . . *sing to us*

of her with violets in her lap.

. . . *most of all*

. . . *wanders*

22.

a task . . .
face . . .
if not, winter . . .
painless . . .

. . . I bid you to sing
of Gongyla, Abanthis, taking up
your lyre, while again desire
        flies around you,

beautiful. For her dress excited you
when you saw it, and I myself rejoice.
For the holy Cyprian herself once
        blamed me

because I prayed . . .
this word . . .
I wish . . .

23.

. . . of love.
. . . for when I see you face to face
. . . even Hermione
. . . to compare you to golden-haired Helen

. . . among mortal women, know this
. . . you could free me from all my cares
. . . on the riverbanks
. . . all through the night

24.

24A.

. . . you will remember,
. . . for we in our youth
did these things,
many, beautiful things.

24C.

. . . we live
. . . opposite
. . . daring
. . . human

24D.

. . . a small voice

25.

. . . left behind
. . . graceful woman

26.

. . . for those
I treat well hurt me
                        most of all.
. . . in vain
. . . you, I wish
. . . suffering
. . . but in my heart
. . . I know this

27.

. . . for once you were a child
. . . come sing these things
. . . talk to us, grant us
                        your favors.

For we are going to a wedding, as you
well know. But as quickly as possible,

send away the virgins.

May the gods have . . .

. . . a road to great Olympus
. . . for mortals

29.

29B.

. . . Lady

29C.

. . . robes
. . . necklaces
. . . for Gorgo

29H.

. . . for Gyrinno

30.

night . . .

virgins . . .
all night long . . .
might sing of the love between you and the bride
with violets in her lap.

But rise up! Call the young men
your own age, so that we may see
less sleep than the . . .
with a clear voice.

31.

He seems to me equal to the gods,
that man who sits opposite you
and listens near
to your sweet voice

and lovely laughter. My heart
begins to flutter in my chest.
When I look at you even for a moment
I can no longer speak.

My tongue fails and a subtle
fire races beneath my skin,
I see nothing with my eyes
        and my ears hum.

Sweat pours from me and a trembling
seizes my whole body. I am greener
than grass and it seems I am a little short
        of dying.

But all must be endured, for even a poor man . . .

32.

. . . who gave me honor by the gift
        of their works

33.

Golden-crowned Aphrodite, if only I
        could win this lot

34.

The stars around the beautiful moon
hide back their radiant form
when she in her fullness shines
                    over the earth.

35.

you either Cyprus or Paphos or Panormus

36.

I long for and seek after

37.

in my dripping pain . . .

May winds and sorrows carry off the one
                    blaming me

38.

you scorch us

39.

a many-colored leather sandal
covered her feet, a beautiful piece of work
from Lydia

40.

and I to you . . . of a white goat

41.

for you lovely ones my thoughts
do not change

42.

their hearts grew cold
and they folded their wings

43.

. . . disturbs the stillness
. . . distress, mind
. . . settles down
. . . but come, beloved ones
. . . for day is near

44.

Cyprus . . .
the herald came . . .
Idaeus, the swift messenger . . .
". . . and the rest of Asia . . . undying glory.
Hector and his companions are bringing the lively-eyed,
graceful Andromache from holy Thebe and ever-flowing
Placia in their ships over the salty sea, along with many
*   golden bracelets*
and perfumed purple robes, beautifully-painted
*   ornaments*
and countless silver cups and ivory."
So he spoke. Quickly Hector's dear father rose up
and the news spread among his friends in the spacious
*   city.*
At once the sons of Ilus yoked mules to the
smooth-running carts, then the whole crowd
of women and maidens with . . . ankles climbed on board.

The daughters of Priam apart . . .
the young men yoked horses to chariots . . .
in great style . . .
charioteers . . .
. . . like the gods
. . . holy together
set out . . . to Ilium
the sweet-sounding flute and the cithara mingled
and the sound of castanets. Maidens sang a holy song
and a wondrous echo reached to the sky . . .
everywhere in the streets was . . .
mixing-bowls and drinking cups . . .
myrrh and cassia and frankincense mingled.
The older women cried out with joy
and all the men erupted in a high-pitched shout
calling on Paean, far-shooting god skilled with the lyre.
They sang in praise of god-like Hector and Andromache.

44Aa.

for golden-haired Phoebus whom the daughter of Coeus
    bore
after she lay with the son of Cronus, whose name is great.
But Artemis swore the great oath of the gods:
"By your head, I will always be a virgin
. . . hunting on the peaks of the mountains.
Come, grant me this for my sake."
. . . and the father of the blessed gods nodded.

The gods call her the hunter, the shooter of deer,
. . . a great title.
. . . Love never approaches her

44Ab.

glorious of the Muses . . .
makes of the Graces . . .
slender . . .
anger not . . .
for mortals . . .

45.

. . . as long as you wish

46.

I will lay down my limbs
on a soft cushion . . .

47.

Love shook my heart
like a mountain wind falling on oaks.

48.

You came and I was longing for you.
You cooled my heart burning with desire.

49.

I loved you, Atthis, once long ago

You seemed to me a small child without grace

50.

For the man who is beautiful is beautiful in appearance,
but the man who is good will be beautiful indeed.

51.

I don't know what I should do. There are two minds in me

52.

I do not expect to touch the sky

53.

Come, rosy-armed holy Graces, daughters of Zeus

54.

. . . who came from heaven wrapped in a purple cloak

55.

But when you die you will lie there and there will be no
    memory
of you nor longing for you after, for you have no share in
    the roses
of Pieria. But you will wander unseen in the house of
    Hades,
flying about among the shadowy dead.

56.

I don't imagine that any girl who has looked on
the light of the sun will ever have such wisdom
as this.

57.

What country girl bewitches your mind . . .
dressed in her country clothes . . .
not knowing how to pull her ragged dress over her ankles?

58.

. . . I pray
. . . now a festival
. . . under the earth
. . . having a gift of honor
. . . as I am now on the earth
. . . taking the sweet-sounding lyre
. . . I sing to the reed-pipe

. . . fleeing
. . . was bitten
. . . gives success to the mouth

. . . beautiful gifts of the violet-laden Muses, children
. . . the sweet-sounding lyre dear to song.
. . . my skin once soft is wrinkled now,
. . . my hair once black has turned to white.
My heart has become heavy, my knees
that once danced nimbly like fawns cannot carry me.
How often I lament these things—but what can be done?

No one who is human can escape old age.
They say that rosy-armed Dawn once took
Tithonus, beautiful and young, carrying him to the
ends of the earth. But in time grey old age still
found him, even though he had an immortal wife.
. . . imagines
. . . might give
I love the pleasures of life . . . and this to me.
Love has given me the brightness and beauty of the sun.

59.

loves . . .
new . . .

60.

. . . meeting
. . . wish
. . . carry out my plan
. . . I call
. . . my heart at once
. . . all you wish to accomplish
. . . to fight for me
. . . persuaded by a wanton woman
. . . for you know well

61.

they became . . .
for not . . .

62.

You were afraid . . .
laurel tree . . .
but everything sweeter . . .
than that . . .
and to those women . . .
a journeyer . . .
I scarcely ever listened . . .
beloved soul . . .
such things now . . .
to come, gentle . . .
you came first, beautiful . . .
and the clothes . . .

63.

Dream of blackness . . .
you come whenever sleep . . .
sweet god, terrible sorrow . . .
keep away the power . . .

but I have hope I will not share . . .
nothing of the blessed ones . . .
for I would not be this way . . .
playthings . . .
but may it happen to me . . .
everything . . .

64.

64A.

for friends . . .
of children . . .
to the gods . . .
shame . . .

65.

for Sappho, you . . .
Cyprus queen . . .
yet great . . .
to all on whom the shining . . .
everywhere glory . . .
and you in Acheron's . . .

67.

67A.

and this . . .
destructive god . . .
truly did not love . . .
now because of . . .
the cause neither . . .
nothing much . . .

67B.

not . . .
these . . .
more . . .
around . . .
love . . .

68.

68A.

. . . for me from the
. . . yet became
. . . her like the gods
. . . sinful

. . . *Andromeda*

. . . *blessed one*

. . . *way*

. . . *did not restrain insolence*

. . . *the sons of Tyndareus*

. . . *kindly*

. . . *innocent no longer*

. . . *Megara*

68B.

. . . *difficult for me*

69.

. . . *sinful*

70.

. . . *I will go*

. . . *of harmony*

. . . *chorus*

. . . *sweet-voiced*

. . . *to all*

71.

. . . Mica

. . . I will not allow you

. . . you chose the love of the house of Penthilus

. . . evil betrayer

. . . sweet song

. . . voice like honey

. . . gentle breezes

. . . wet with dew

73.

73A.

. . . Aphrodite

. . . sweet words of love

. . . cast away

. . . having

. . . sits

. . . dew

74.

74A.

. . . goatherd
. . . roses

74B.

. . . longing

74C.

. . . sweat

76.

. . . I want
. . . to hold

78.

. . . not
. . . longing
. . . suddenly

. . . blossom
. . . longing

80.

. . . all
. . . but not the same

81.

. . . reject
. . . as quickly as possible
But you, Dica, weave lovely garlands in your hair,
tying stems of anise with your soft hands.
For the blessed Graces prefer to look on those adorned
with flowers and turn away from those without crowns.

82.

82A.

Mnasidica more finely shaped than tender Gyrinno . . .

82B.

. . . and
. . . nothing
. . . but now
. . . not
. . . more finely shaped

83.

. . . right now
. . . again
. . . for

84.

. . . delicate
. . . Artemis

85.

85B.

. . . like the old man

86.

. . . peaceful
. . . aegis-bearing
. . . Cytherea I pray
. . . holding my heart
. . . hear my prayer if ever
. . . leaving behind
. . . to my
. . . difficult

87.

87A.

. . . rumor
. . . lock of hair
. . . together
. . . human

87B.

. . . worry

87C.

. . . daring

87D.

. . . youth

87E.

. . . queen

87F.

. . . for you

88.

88AB.

. . . loosen
. . . you would be willing
. . . few
. . . to be carried
. . . me . . . more sweetly
. . . you yourself know
. . . someone would say
. . . for I will love
. . . as long as there is in me
. . . will care
. . . I say that I have been a faithful lover

. . . painful

. . . bitter

. . . but know this

. . . whatever you

. . . I will love

. . . for

. . . of arrows

91.

. . . never have I found you more harmful, Irana

92.

robe . . .

saffron . . .

purple robe . . .

cloaks . . .

crowns . . .

beautiful . . .

purple . . .

93.

. . . I have
. . . of virgins

94.

. . . "I honestly wish I were dead."
Weeping she left me

with many tears and said this:
"Oh, this has turned out so badly for us, Sappho.
Truly, I leave you against my will."

And I answered her:
"Be happy and go—and remember me.
for you know how much we loved you.

But if not, I want to remind
you . . .
. . . and the good times we had.

For many crowns of violets
and roses and . . .
. . . you put on by my side,

and many woven garlands
made from flowers
around your soft throat,

and with much perfume
costly . . .
fit for a queen, you anointed yourself.

And on a soft bed
delicate . . .
you let loose your desire.

And not any . . . nor any
holy place nor . . .
from which we were absent.

No grove . . . no dance
. . . no sound

95.

Gongyla . . .
surely some sign . . .
especially for children . . .
came in . . .
I said: "O master . . .
not the blessed . . .

I take no pleasure . . .
a kind of longing has seized me to die
and see the dewy banks of Acheron
covered in lotus . . .

96.

. . . Sardis
. . . often turning her thoughts to this

. . . you like a goddess
and in your song she delighted most of all.

Now she stands out among
the women of Lydia,
like the rosy-fingered moon after sunset

surpasses all the stars. Its light
spreads alike over the salty sea
and fields rich in flowers.

The dew is poured forth in beauty,
roses bloom along with tender chevil
and flowering melilot.

She wanders to and fro remembering
gentle Atthis, and her tender
heart is consumed.

to go there . . .
much . . .
says . . .

For us it isn't easy to rival the goddesses
in lovely form . . .

. . . love
. . . Aphrodite

. . . poured nectar
from golden cups . . .
. . . with hands Persuasion

. . . to the Geraesteum
. . . beloved

97.

flying about . . .
ivory . . .

98.

98A.

For my mother used to say
that when she was young it was
a great ornament if someone had her hair
bound in a purple headband.

But for a girl whose hair
is yellower than
a flaming torch . . .

crowns adorned with
blooming flowers.
Recently a decorated headband

. . . from Sardis
. . . cities

98B.

But for you, Cleis, I have no beautiful headband
nor do I know how to get one.
But the one in Mytiline . . .

. . . to have
. . . adorned

. . . these things of the family of Cleanax
. . . exile
. . . memories dreadfully wasted away

100.

. . . and covered her completely with soft woven cloth

101.

. . . hand cloths
. . . purple
. . . sent from Phocaea
. . . expensive gifts

102.

Truly, sweet mother, I cannot weave on the loom,
for I am overcome with desire for a boy because of slender
*   Aphrodite.*

103.

1. . . . *for speak*
2. . . . *the bride with beautiful feet*
3. . . . *the child of Zeus with violets in her lap*
4. . . . *putting away anger, the one with violets in her lap*
5. . . . *holy Graces and Muses of Pieria*
6. . . . *when songs, the mind*
7. . . . *hearing a clear song*
8. . . . *bridegroom, vexing*
9. . . . *her hair, putting down the lyre*
10. . . . *golden-sandaled Dawn*

103Aa.

. . . *small*
. . . *many*
. . . *many*
. . . *their*
. . . *Gorgo*

103Ab.

. . . *to Cypris*

103B.

. . . chamber
. . . bride with beautiful feet
. . . now
. . . for me

103Ca.

. . . to carry
. . . Archeanassa
. . . once in the past
. . . beloved

103Cb.

. . . they heard
. . . maidens

104.

104A.

*Evening, you gather together all that shining Dawn has
    scattered.
You bring back the sheep, you bring back the goat, you
    bring back
        the child to its mother.*

104B.

. . . most beautiful of all the stars

105.

105A.

*. . . like the sweet apple that grows red on the lofty branch,
at the very top of the highest bough. The apple-pickers
    have forgotten it
—no, not forgotten, but they could not reach it.*

105B.

*. . . like the hyacinth shepherds tread underfoot
in the mountains, and on the ground the purple flower*

106.

superior, as the singer of Lesbos to those of other lands

107.

Do I still long for my virginity?

108.

O beautiful one, O graceful one

109.

We will give, says the father

110.

The door-keeper's feet are as long as seven outstretched
    arms,
and his sandals are made from five ox-hides,
ten cobblers labored hard to make them.

111.

Raise high the roof—
Hymenaeus!
Raise it up, carpenters—
Hymenaeus!
The bridegroom is coming, the equal of Ares,
and he's much bigger than a big man.

112.

Blessed bridegroom, your wedding has been accomplished
just as you prayed and you have the maiden bride you
        desired.

Your form is graceful and your eyes . . .
honey-sweet. Love pours over your lovely face . . .
. . . Aphrodite has greatly honored you

113.

            for never,
bridegroom, was there another girl like this one.

114.

"Virginity, virginity, where have you gone? You've deserted me!"
"Never again will I come to you, never again will I come."

115.

To what, dear bridegroom, can I in handsomeness compare you?
To a slender sapling most of all I do compare you.

116.

Farewell, bride, farewell, much-honored bridegroom.

117.

May you fare well, bride, and may the bridegroom fare well.

117A.

of polished doors

118.

Come, divine lyre, speak to me
and become a voice

119.

a handkerchief dripping

120

But I am not one of those with spiteful passions.
I have a gentle heart.

121.

But if I am your friend, choose the bed of someone younger.
For I cannot bear to live with you if I am the older one.

122.

so delicate a girl picking flowers

123.

just now golden-sandaled Dawn

124.

and you yourself, Calliope

125.

I myself used to weave crowns of flowers

126.

May you sleep on the bosom of your gentle companion.

127.

Come here again, Muses, leaving the golden . . .

128.

Come here now, tender Graces and Muses with beautiful
   hair.

129.

129A.

but you have forgotten me

129B.

or you love another more than me

130.

Once again limb-loosening Love makes me tremble,
that bittersweet, irresistible creature.

131.

But Atthis, it's become hateful to you to think
of me, and you've flown off to Andromeda.

132.

I have a beautiful child who is like golden flowers
in form, my beloved Cleis, for whom
I would not take all of Lydia or lovely . . .

133.

133A.

Andromeda has a fine revenge

133B.

Sappho, why? Aphrodite rich in blessings . . .

134.

I talked with you in a dream, Cyprus-born

135.

Why, Irana, does Pandion's daughter, the swallow, me . . .

136.

Messenger of spring, the nightingale with a voice of
*   longing*

137.

"I want to say something to you, but
shame prevents me . . ."
"But if you had a desire for things that are good or
*   beautiful*
and your tongue weren't busy stirring up evil,
shame would not lower your eyes,
but you would speak about what is just."

138.

Stand before me, dear one,
and spread forth the grace in your eyes.

139.

the gods . . . quickly, the one without tears

140.

"*Delicate Adonis is dying, Cytherea—what should we
    do?*"
"*Beat your breasts, girls, and tear your clothes.*"

141.

*But there a bowl of ambrosia
had been mixed.
And Hermes taking the jug poured wine for the gods.
They all held
drinking-cups
and offered libations and prayed for all good things
for the bridegroom.*

142.

Leto and Niobe were beloved companions

143.

. . . and golden chickpeas were growing on the banks

144.

. . . they have had their fill indeed of Gorgo

145.

Don't move small stones

146.

I want neither the honey nor the bee

147.

Someone, I say, will remember us in time to come

148.

Wealth without virtue is no harmless neighbor,
but a mixture of both brings the height of happiness.

149.

when all night long it pulls them down

150.

It is not right in the house of those serving the Muses
for there to be lamenting. That would not be fitting for us.

151.

and on the eyes the black sleep of night

152.

mingled with all kinds of colors

153.

the virgin with the sweet voice

154.

The moon in its fullness appeared,
and when the women took their places around the altar . . .

155.

I wish the daughter of the house of Polyanax much joy

156.

far more sweet-sounding than a lyre . . .
more golden than gold . . .

157.

. . . Lady Dawn

158.

. . . when anger is swelling in the chest
to guard against the vainly-barking tongue

159.

. . . you and my servant Love

160.

. . . and now for my companions
I will sing these songs beautifully

161.

guard her . . . bridegrooms . . . kings of cities

162.

with what eyes?

163.

my beloved one

164.

she calls her son

165.

That man seems to himself . . .

166.

They say that Leda once found
an egg, hyacinth-colored, covered . . .

167.

. . . far whiter than an egg

168.

Oh, for Adonis

168A.

who loves children more than Gello

168B.

The moon has set
and the Pleiades. It's the middle
of the night and time goes by.
I lie here alone.

168C.

the earth is adorned
with many crowns . . .

169.

I would lead

169A.

wedding gifts

170.

Aiga

171.

innocent

172.

pain-giver

173.

a vine growing up a tree

174.

channel

175.

dawn

176.

lyre

177.

transparent dress

179.

purse

180.

the Holder

181.

fordable

182.

I might go

183.

downrushing

184.

danger

185.

honey-voiced

186.

Medea

187.

of the Muses

188.

weaver of tales

189.

soda

190.

many–skilled

191.

celery

192.

golden–knobbed cups

The Brothers Poem

*But you are always chattering that Charaxus is coming
with a full ship. These things, I suppose, Zeus
knows and all the other gods. But you should not*
worry about them.

*Instead send me and ask me to call on
and make many prayers to Queen Hera
that Charaxus return here,*
steering his ship,

and find us safe and sound. Everything else,
all of it, let us leave to the gods.
For fair weather comes quickly
> *from great storms.*

Those to whom the king of Olympus wishes
to send a helpful spirit to banish toils,
these will be happy
> *and rich in blessings.*

And we—if someday his head is freed from labor
and Larichus becomes a gentleman of leisure
—may we be delivered quickly
> *from great heaviness of heart.*

The Cypris Poem

How can a person not be so often distressed,
Queen Cypris, about someone
you want so much to make
> *your own?*

ACKNOWLEDGMENTS

I'M DEEPLY GRATEFUL to all the people who helped make this book possible. First, to the Institute for Advanced Study in Princeton, where I first began my research, and to Luther College, which allowed me a sabbatical to pursue my work. Thanks also to the kind scholars at the Egypt Exploration Society and the Sackler Library at Oxford University for all their help with ancient papyri and the Egyptian site of Oxyrhynchus. My gratitude as well to my guides in Egypt and on the beautiful Greek island of Lesbos. The book would not have been possible without Joëlle Delbourgo and the wonderful editors and staff at W. W. Norton, especially Jill Bialosky, Angie Shih, and Stephanie Hiebert. Thanks finally to my wife, Alison, who listened patiently to yet another of my translations from the original Greek of Sappho and offered her advice on so many aspects of the book.

NOTES

INTRODUCTION

xi "Sappho: Daughter of Simon": *Suda* S 107, in *Greek Lyric I: Sappho and Alcaeus*, ed. David Campbell (Cambridge, MA: Harvard University Press, 2002), 4–7.

xii In ancient times it had been known as Oxyrhynchus: The best sources for the ancient city of Oxyrhynchus and the modern excavations there beginning with Grenfell and Hunt are Peter Parsons, *City of the Sharp-Nosed Fish: Greek Lives in Roman Egypt* (London: Weidenfeld & Nicolson, 2007); and A. K. Bowman et al., eds., *Oxyrhynchus: A City and Its Texts* (London: Egypt Exploration Society, 2007).

xiv "And Jesus said, 'I stood in the middle'": Oxyrhynchus papyrus 1, lines 11–17. These verses were published by Grenfell and Hunt in *The Oxyrhynchus Papyri* (London: Egypt Exploration Fund, 1898), 1:1–3. They are better known today as part of Saying 28 of the Greek-language fragments of the original Coptic *Gospel of Thomas* (see Bart D. Ehrman and Zlatko Plese, eds., *The Apocryphal Gospels* [Oxford: Oxford University Press, 2011], 342–43).

xv "... Nereids, grant that": From Sappho, Poem 5 (Oxyrhynchus papyrus 1, lines 1–8), in Campbell, *Greek Lyric I*, 60–63. The Oxyrhynchus papyri may be found online at http://www.papyrology .ox.ac.uk/POxy.

xvii They belonged to the first woman poet: More precisely, the first

241

woman poet whose work has survived as a part of the continuous literary tradition. Undoubtedly, many female poets preceded Sappho in human history, but their songs have been lost. One exception is the Sumerian priestess Enheduanna, who lived in the latter centuries of the third millennium BC, but her beautiful hymns were unknown until the twentieth century. See Betty De Shong Meador, *Inanna: Lady of the Largest Heart* (Austin: University of Texas Press, 2000).

xvii "It is not very likely that we shall find": Grenfell and Hunt, *Oxyrhynchus Papyri*, 1:vi.

xviii "When I look at you even for a moment": Sappho, Poem 31.

xx "Deathless Aphrodite on your dazzling throne": Sappho, Poem 1.

xxiii "And on a soft bed": Sappho, Poem 94.

xxiii ". . . for when I see you face to face": Sappho, Poem 23.

CHAPTER ONE: CHILDHOOD

1 "Don't worry if the others return": Oxyrhynchus papyrus 4.744, http://www.papyrology.ox.ac.uk/POxy.

2 Infant mortality is notoriously difficult: The best introduction to childhood in ancient Greece and Rome is Judith Evans Grubbs and Tim Parkin, eds., *The Oxford Handbook of Childhood and Education in the Classical World* (Oxford: Oxford University Press, 2013). For infant mortality and child exposure, see Robert Garland, *The Greek Way of Life* (Ithaca, NY: Cornell University Press, 1990), 84–93, 108–113; Mary R. Lefkowitz and Maureen B. Fant, eds., *Women's Life in Greece and Rome: A Sourcebook in Translation* (Baltimore: Johns Hopkins University Press, 1992), 187; Nancy Demand, *Birth, Death, and Motherhood in Classical Greece* (Baltimore: Johns Hopkins University Press, 1994), 5–8; and Robert Garland, *The Greek Way of Death* (Ithaca, NY: Cornell University Press, 2001), 77–88.

3 "If you have a son you raise him": Posidippus frag. 11, in *Posidippi*

pellaei quae supersunt omnia, eds. C. Austin and G. Bastianini (Milan: LED Edizioni Universitarie, 2002).

3 **a child was not a member of its family:** See Jenifer Neils and John H. Oakley, eds., *Coming of Age in Ancient Greece* (New Haven, CT: Yale University Press, 2003), 143–45. The description of the feast at the Amphidromia ritual is from comedy writer Ephippus (T. Kock, *Comicorum atticorum fragmenta* [Leipzig: Teubner, 1884], 2:251–3). The Echinos relief is discussed in Neils and Oakley, *Coming of Age*, 145.

4 **Artemis, a virgin goddess praised by Sappho:** Artemis is mentioned by Sappho in Poems 44A and 84. Philostratus (*Life of Apollonius of Tyana* 1.30, in *Greek Lyric I: Sappho and Alcaeus*, ed. David Campbell [Cambridge, MA: Harvard University Press, 2002], 20–21), also says that Sappho wrote poems to Artemis.

4 **Sappho's mother was Cleis:** Oxyrhynchus papyrus 1800, in Campbell, *Greek Lyric I*, 2–5; *Suda* S 107, in Campbell, *Greek Lyric I*, 4–7. No one is certain what Sappho's name means. The Greek word *sappheirinos* means "blue like lapis lazuli," but the similarity to the poet's name is probably a coincidence. She does not, in fact, call herself *Sappho* in her own poems (1, 65, 94, 133), but *Psappho*, a spelling preserved by scribes in the papyri of Egypt. It's possible that Sappho's name isn't Greek at all, but a borrowing from one of the ancient languages across the narrow strait separating Lesbos from Asia.

5 **"For my mother used to say":** Sappho, Poem 98A.

5 **Later writers list no fewer than eight:** Oxyrhynchus papyrus 1800; *Suda* S 107; Aelian, *Miscellaneous Histories* 12.19. A man from Mytilene on Lesbos, Erigyius, who shared one of the possible names of Sappho's father, was a general in the army of Alexander the Great (Arrian, *Anabasis* 3.11.10).

5 **"Six birthdays had passed for me":** Ovid, *Heroides* 15.61–62.

5 **three brothers, named Erygius, Larichus, and Charaxus:** Two papyri from Egypt (Oxyrhynchus papyri 1800 and 2506) list the brothers as Erygius, Larichus, and Charaxus, as does the later *Suda*

encyclopedia (*Suda* S 107). See also the newly discovered "Brothers Poem," which lists Charaxus and Larichus.

6 **The most likely place is Eresus:** For Eresus, *Suda* S 107; *Palatine Anthology* 7.407, in Campbell, *Greek Lyric I*, 48–49. For Mytilene, Oxyrhynchus papyrus 1800; *Suda* S 108, in Campbell, *Greek Lyric I*, 6–7.

6 **The year of Sappho's birth:** Ancient evidence is in Strabo 13.2.3; Athenaeus, *Learned Diners* 13.598bc–599cd; *Suda* S 107; Parian Marble ep. 36, in Campbell, *Greek Lyric I*, 8–9; Eusebius, *Chronicle* Ol. 45.1, in Campbell, *Greek Lyric I*, 8–9. See G. O. Hutchinson, *Greek Lyric Poetry: A Commentary on Selected Larger Pieces* (Oxford: Oxford University Press, 2001), 139–40.

7 **Sappho lived during a revolutionary period:** For a survey of the period, see L. H. Jeffery, *Archaic Greece: The City States c. 700–500 B.C.* (London: Methuen, 1978); Anthony Snodgrass, *Archaic Greece: The Age of Experiment* (Berkeley: University of California Press, 1981); Nigel Spencer, "Early Lesbos between East and West: A 'Grey Area' of Aegean Archaeology," *Annual of the British School at Athens* 90 (1995): 269–306; Jonathan M. Hall, *A History of the Archaic Greek World: ca. 1200–479 BCE* (Malden, MA: Wiley-Blackwell, 2014).

8 **Boys and girls played with toys:** See Neils and Oakley, *Coming of Age*, 264–82.

8 **"The children put purple reins on you":** *Palatine Anthology* 6.312.

10 **"Evening, you gather together":** Sappho, Poem 104A.

10 **"From his earliest years":** *Homeric Problems* 1 = D. A. Russell and D. Konstan, eds., *Heraclitus: Homeric Problems* (Atlanta: Society of Biblical Literature, 2005), 2.

11 **The Greek historian Xenophon:** Xenophon, *Oeconomicus* 7.

11 **Many of the images of female children:** For example, Neils and Oakley, *Coming of Age*, 61, 119.

11 **There were even wool-working contests:** Ibid., 118.

11 **Girls in the military-dominated city of Sparta:** Xenophon, *Constitution of the Spartans* 1.4.

11   As an aristocratic girl: A fragmentary papyrus commentary of the first or second century AD does claim that Sappho was a good and industrious housekeeper (Oxyrhynchus papyrus 2506, frag. 48).

12   aside from garlands of flowers: Sappho, Poem 125.

12   Plato reportedly had two women: Diogenes Laertius, *Lives of Famous Philosophers* 3.46.

12   to think of Sappho as the leader of a school: Marguerite Johnson, *Sappho* (Bristol, England: Bristol Classical Press, 2007), 13–14.

13   One ancient Greek writer even claimed: Menaechmus in Athenaeus, *Learned Diners* 14.635b.

13   a *plectrum*, which Sappho also reportedly invented: *Suda* S 107.

14   "You seemed to me a small child without grace": Sappho, Poem 49. It is quoted by Plutarch (*Dialogue on Love* 751d), who says that Sappho is addressing a girl too young for marriage.

14   ". . . you will remember": Sappho, Poem 24A.

14   ". . . into a deep wave": Erinna, *Distaff* 5–21.

16   Sappho mentions a similar monster: Sappho, Poem 168A.

16   "my knees that once danced nimbly": Sappho, Poem 58.

17   "I sing of the light of Agido": Alcman, *Partheneion* 1.39–49.

18   "With desire that makes my limbs loose": Ibid., 3.61–72.

19   "At seven I became Bearer of Secret Things": Aristophanes, *Lysistrata* 643–46. See Mark Golden, *Children and Childhood in Classical Athens* (Baltimore: Johns Hopkins University Press, 1990), 76–79; Neils and Oakley, *Coming of Age*, 149–53.

CHAPTER TWO: WEDDING SONGS

23   "Let your bride be": Hesiod, *Works and Days* 698–99.

23   The Byzantine *Suda* encyclopedia says: *Suda* S 107, in *Greek Lyric I: Sappho and Alcaeus*, ed. David Campbell (Cambridge, MA: Harvard University Press, 2002), 4–7. We know of several ancient comedies featuring Sappho as the main character that date from as early as the fifth century BC. See David A. Campbell, *Greek Lyric*

Poetry (Bristol, England: Bristol Classical Press, 1990), 5n4; Marguerite Johnson, *Sappho* (Bristol, England: Bristol Classical Press, 2007), 23.

24　The poet Hesiod: Hesiod, *Works and Days* 695–96. For the ideal age of marriage for men and women in ancient Greece, see Robert Garland, *The Greek Way of Life* (Ithaca, NY: Cornell University Press, 1990), 210–13.

25　The philosophers Plato and Aristotle: Plato, *Laws* 6.785b; Aristotle, *Politics* 7.1335a.

26　It was also widely believed: Soranos, *Gynecology* 1.33.

26　A Hippocratic treatise on illnesses: Hippocrates, *Illnesses Affecting Virgins* 1. See Garland, *Greek Way of Life*, 168–70.

27　a beautiful and clever princess named Nausicaa: Homer, *Odyssey* 6.273–89.

28　"'Don't refuse me, dear . . .'": Archilochus frag. 196a.

29　"I urge you not to slip and fall, my dears": Aeschylus, *Suppliants* 996–1005.

29　But it's Sappho herself: For an excellent discussion, see Johnson, *Sappho*, 112–21. It is possible that these two fragments come from different poems, but it seems unlikely.

30　". . . like the sweet apple that grows red": Sappho, Poem 105A.

30　". . . like the hyacinth shepherds tread underfoot": Sappho, Poem 105B. Demetrius, *On Style* 140.

31　"'Virginity, virginity, where have you gone?'": Sappho, Poem 114. Demetrius, *On Style* 140.

32　An intriguing passage by: Herodotus 1.93. Herodotus also claims that all Lydian women of the common class worked as prostitutes to earn money for their dowries.

32　The sixth-century aristocrat Callias: Herodotus 6.122.

32　Helen of Troy: Euripides, *Iphegenia at Aulis* 68–69.

32　"Come now, you suitors": Homer, *Odyssey* 21.73–77.

34　"O fortunate son of Laertes": Ibid., 24.192–98.

34　"A man couldn't gain anything better": Hesiod, *Works and Days* 702–6.

35 "In the beginning Zeus created": Semonides 7.

36 "For me it would be better": Homer, *Iliad* 6.410–12, 429–30.

37 "Mighty goddess, do not be angry with me": Homer, *Odyssey* 5.215–20.

37 "FATHER: I give you this girl": Menander, *Perikeiromene* 435–37. See Garland, *Greek Way of Life*, 217–18.

38 In Homeric times: For example, Homer, *Odyssey* 16.390–92.

38 but the scene is not found in Homer: Homer does include a brief description of a wedding in a passage portraying the shield of Achilles (*Iliad* 18.491–95).

39 "Cyprus . . . / the herald came . . .": Sappho, Poem 44. See Johnson, *Sappho*, 61–66, 102–5.

43 ". . . for once you were a child": Sappho, Poem 27.

44 "No mortal may go soaring to the heavens": Alcman 1.16.

45 "Truly, sweet mother, I cannot weave": Sappho, Poem 102.

46 ". . . bride with beautiful feet": Sappho, Poem 103B. See Johnson, *Sappho*, 105–6.

46 but in the earlier Greek poetic tradition: Homer, *Iliad* 14.186; Hesiod, *Theogony*, 507.

46 "Blessed bridegroom, your wedding": Sappho, Poem 112.

47 "for never, / bridegroom, was there another girl like this one": Sappho, Poem 113.

47 "To what, dear bridegroom": Sappho, Poem 115.

48 "Farewell, bride": Sappho, Poem 116. See also Poem 117.

48 "loosen the pure virgin's girdle": Alcaeus, Poem 42.

49 "Sappho makes cheap fun": Demetrius, *On Style* 167.

49 a Byzantine churchman was still complaining: Michael of Italy, *Address to Michael Oxites* (see Eva-Maria Voigt, ed., *Sappho et Alcaeus: Fragmenta* [Amsterdam: Athenaeum, 1971], 155 Campbell, *Greek Lyric Poetry*, 140–41).

49 "Raise high the roof—": Sappho, Poem 111.

50 "The door-keeper's feet are as long as": Sappho, Poem 110.

50 "virgins . . . / all night long . . .": Sappho, Poem 30. See Johnson, *Sappho*, 120–21.

52 "The rest of the Trojan women": Homer, *Odyssey* 4.257–64.

52 "You came along, Helen": Ibid., 4.273–79.

53 he offers Achilles seven female slaves from Lesbos: Homer, *Iliad* 9.128–30.

54 This is followed by more practical advice: Plutarch, *Advice on Marriage* 1, 9, 11, 18, 19, 35.

55 "We have prostitutes for sexual pleasure": Pseudo-Demosthenes 59.122.

55 "Surely you don't think men have children": Xenophon, *Memorabilia* 2.2.4.

56 A woman who committed adultery: Demosthenes 59.86–87.

CHAPTER THREE: A MOTHER'S LOVE

57 "I have a beautiful child": Sappho, Poem 132.

57 a fragmentary papyrus scroll: Oxyrhynchus papyrus 1800, frag. 1, http://www.papyrology.ox.ac.uk/POxy.

57 the Byzantine *Suda* encyclopedia: *Suda* S 107, in *Greek Lyric I: Sappho and Alcaeus*, ed. David Campbell (Cambridge, MA: Harvard University Press, 2002), 4–7.

58 "For my mother used to say": Sappho, Poems 98A and 98B.

60 the same Greek word used by Homer: For example, *Iliad* 1.197 (Achilles); *Odyssey* 13.399 (Odysseus).

60 "I have a beautiful child": Sappho, Poem 132.

60 with Homer reserving it only for sons: For example, describing Telemachus in *Odyssey* 2.365.

61 "About Cleis later on": David A. Campbell, *Greek Lyric Poetry* (Bristol, England: Bristol Classical Press, 1990), 196–97.

63 A woman's primary role in ancient Greece: For this section, I am indebted to the excellent primary sources on and discussion of conception, pregnancy, and childbirth in Robert Garland, *The Greek Way of Life* (Ithaca, NY: Cornell University Press, 1990), 17–105.

63 "The mother is not the begetter of the child": Aeschylus, *Eumenides* 658–59.

63 One ancient medical text tells the story: Soranus, *Gynecology* 1.39.

64 Aristotle also advised: Aristotle, *History of Animals* 7.3.

64 Insertion into the vagina: *Superfetation* 32–39.

64 Other aids to conception: Soranos, *Gynecology* 1.38–41; Hesiod, *Works and Days* 735ff.

64 It was also believed that men: Aristotle, *Generation of Animals* 1.718.

65 "Nature . . . takes a portion from each partner": Plutarch, *Advice on Marriage* 20.

66 "During intercourse when a man": Soranus, *Gynecology* 1.61.

66 One Greek physician: *Nature of the Child* 13.

67 Various kinds of ointments: See, for example, Soranus, *Gynecology* 1.61.

67 Other doctors prescribed a meal: *Nature of Women* 98.

68 "For abortions are more painful than birth": *Illnesses of Women* 1.72.

68 Soranus recommended: Soranus, *Gynecology* 1.64–65.

68 "When, as so often happens": *Illnesses of Women* 1.67.

69 Carved in stone: See P. J. Rhodes and Robin Osborne, eds. *Greek Historical Inscriptions 404–323 BC* (Oxford: Oxford University Press, 2007), 102.10–22. Another inscription (102.3–9) from the same site reports a five-year pregnancy.

69 One medical text claimed: *Nature of the Child* 12–29.

70 to avoid stepping over a raven's egg: Pliny, *Natural History* 30.44.

71 the poet Hesiod advised: Hesiod, *Works and Days* 780–813.

72 "I would rather stand in battle": Euripides, *Medea* 250.

72 "Why would I want to go to bed?": Plutarch, *Advice on Marriage* 39.

73 A midwife would apply: Soranus, *Gynecology* 1.56–57.

74 In Sparta these women: Plutarch, *Lycurgus* 27.

74 The gruesome details of the procedure: *Cutting Up the Fetus* 1; Garland, *Greek Way of Life*, 76–77.

74 the physician Soranus recommended: Soranus, *Gynecology* 4.9.

75 "The son of Cichesias dedicates": Garland, *Greek Way of Life*, 83.

75 "It's the woman who becomes pregnant": Xenophon, *Memorabilia* 2.2.5.

76 One such image is from: Rhode Island School of Design Museum of Art, Providence, 25.088; Jenifer Neils and John H. Oakley, eds., *Coming of Age in Ancient Greece* (New Haven, CT: Yale University Press, 2003), 236.

76 Another vase from the same century: British Museum, London, E 396; Neils and Oakley, *Coming of Age*, 237.

77 A small Athenian terra-cotta figurine: Museum of Fine Arts, Boston, 02.38; Neils and Oakley, *Coming of Age*, 239.

77 One of the most charming: Royal Museums of Art and History, Brussels, A 890; Neils and Oakley, *Coming of Age*, 240–41.

77 a fifth-century-BC terra-cotta figurine: Museum of Fine Arts, Boston, H.10.7; Neils and Oakley, *Coming of Age*, 112, 257.

79 "Oh, my dear Orestes": Aeschylus, *Libation Bearers* 749–60.

80 but the relationship between: See Nancy Demand, *Birth, Death, and Motherhood in Classical Greece* (Baltimore: Johns Hopkins University Press, 1994), 15–17.

81 "Leaving two young daughters": *Inscriptiones Graecae* II² 12335.

81 ". . . hurry and write to me": Oxyrhynchus papyrus 930.

82 "She stepped up close to him": Homer, *Odyssey* 6.59–67.

CHAPTER FOUR: FAMILY MATTERS

85 "ANTIGONE: Will you help": Sophocles, *Antigone* 44–50.

88 "She had three brothers, Erigyius, Larichus, and Charaxus": Oxyrhynchus papyrus 1800, frag. 1, http://www.papyrology.ox.ac.uk/POxy.

88 "She had three brothers, Larichus, Charaxus, and Erigyius": *Suda* S 107, in *Greek Lyric I: Sappho and Alcaeus*, ed. David Campbell (Cambridge, MA: Harvard University Press, 2002), 4–7.

88 "Cha(raxus) ... / and ... / dearest ... (Lari)chus ...": Oxyrhynchus papyrus 2506, frag. 48.

89 "The lovely Sappho often praises": Athenaeus, *Learned Diners* 10.425a.

89 "It was the custom, as Sappho says": Ancient commentator on Homer's *Iliad*, 20.234.

89 as Nehemiah did for the Persian King: Neh. 2:1.

89 In the Archaic period: An excellent summary of the Archaic political history of Lesbos can be found in A. R. Burn, *The Lyric Age of Greece* (London: Edward Arnold, 1978), 226–46.

90 Aristotle says Megacles: Aristotle, *Politics* 1311b.

92 "But Potbelly didn't": Alcaeus, Poem 129.

93 "... Mica / ... I will not allow you": Sappho, Poem 71.

94 "But for you, Cleis": Sappho, Poem 98B.

95 The Parian Marble, a chronology: Parian Marble 36 (see p. 1955, 224–25), in *Greek Lyric I: Sappho and Alcaeus*, ed. David Campbell (Cambridge, MA: Harvard University Press, 2002), 8–9.

96 Sappho mentions Panormus: Sappho, Poem 35.

96 We know from the first-century-BC Roman orator Cicero: Cicero, *Against Verres* 2.4.125–27.

98 "... hand cloths / ... purple": Sappho, Poem 101.

99 goods from Lydia: Sappho, Poems 39, 98, 132.

99 incense from southern Arabia: Sappho, Poem 44.

100 "... Nereids, grant that": Sappho, Poem 5.

102 "of Doricha ... / commands, for not ...": Sappho, Poem 7.

102 "... that he atone for his past mistakes": Sappho, Poem 15.

103 The historian Herodotus: Herodotus 2.135.

103 The Greek geographer Strabo: Strabo 17.1.33.

103 "Doricha, your bones fell asleep long ago ...": Athenaeus, *Learned Diners* 13.596c–d.

104 There is a hint: Ovid, *Letters of the Heroines* 15.63–70.

105 "But you are always chattering": Sappho, "The Brothers Poem."

107 "Leave everything else to the gods": Horace, *Ode* 1.9.

CHAPTER FIVE: LOVING WOMEN

109 "This is why we have": Plato, *Symposium* 191.

109 There is no word for "homosexual": For an introduction to same-sex relationships in classical times and the variety of modern scholarly opinions on the subject, see Thomas K. Hubbard, ed., *Homosexuality in Greece and Rome: A Sourcebook of Basic Documents* (Berkeley: University of California Press, 2003), 1–20.

111 "In youth you can sleep": Theognis 1063–64.

111 "Although your first down": Strato, *AP* 12.10.

111 The poet Archilochus: Archilochus frag. 25.1–5.

112 "Cosmos, the slave of Equitia": *Corpus Inscriptionum Latinarum* 4.1825.

112 One graffito of Jewish or Christian origin: Ibid., 4.4976.

112 "The girls from Samos": Asclepiades, *Palatine Anthology* 5.207.

112 Archilochus, who mocked sexual relations: Archilochus frag. 294.

113 "Love was so esteemed among them": Plutarch, *Lycurgus* 18.4.

113 The noted physician Hippocrates: Hippocrates, *On Regimen* 1.29.

113 as did Plato in the famous parable: Plato, *Symposium* 189–93.

113 "We hear interesting things": Lucian, *Dialogues of the Courtesans* 5.

114 "I implore you, Good Messenger": *Papyri Graecae Magicae* 32.

115 Root of gloomy darkness: *Supplementum Magicum* 1.42.

116 "Deathless Aphrodite on your dazzling throne": Sappho, Poem 1.

119 Love charms and magic spells: For Sappho's use of magic charms in her poetry, see J. C. B. Petropoulos, "Sappho the Sorceress—Another Look at Fr. 1," *Zeitschrift für Papyrologie und Epigraphik* 97 (1993): 43–56; Charles Segal, "Eros and Incantation: Sappho and Oral Poetry," in *Reading Sappho: Contemporary Approaches*, ed. Ellen Greene (Berkeley: University of California Press, 1996), 58–75. For spells and magic in the ancient world in general, see John G. Gager, *Curse Tablets and Binding Spells from the Ancient World* (Oxford: Oxford University Press, 1992); Hans Dieter Betz, ed., *The Greek Magical Papyri in Translation* (Chicago: University of

NOTES

Chicago Press, 1992); Georg Luck, *Arcana Mundi: Magic and the Occult in the Greek and Roman Worlds* (Baltimore: Johns Hopkins University Press, 2006).

119 Homer even sings of incantations: Homer, *Odyssey* 19.457–58.

120 "He seems to me equal to the gods": Sappho, Poem 31.

121 "Sappho each time uses the emotions": Pseudo-Longinus, *On the Sublime* 10.1–3.

121 Readers of this poem for two thousand years: For a discussion of the poem, see Denys Page, *Sappho and Alcaeus: An Introduction to the Study of Ancient Lesbian Poetry* (Oxford: Clarendon, 1965), 19–33; Jane McIntosh Snyder, *Lesbian Desire in the Lyrics of Sappho* (New York: Columbia University Press, 1997), 27–38; G. O. Hutchinson, *Greek Lyric Poetry: A Commentary on Selected Larger Pieces* (Oxford: Oxford University Press, 2001), 168–77; Marguerite Johnson, *Sappho* (Bristol, England: Bristol Classical Press, 2007), 79–84.

123 "raw physicality": Snyder, *Lesbian Desire*, 29.

123 Homer uses the same Greek word: Homer, *Odyssey* 22.298.

123 as does Alcaeus when he says: Alcaeus, Poem 283, though the text here is uncertain.

123 using the same word that Homer does: Homer, *Iliad* 8.403.

124 classical scholar Eleanor Irwin: Eleanor Irwin, *Colour Terms in Greek Poetry* (Toronto: Hakkert, 1974), 31–78. See also Robert J. Edgeworth, "Sappho Fr. 31.14," *Acta Classica* 27 (1984): 121–24; Snyder, *Lesbian Desire*, 33.

125 "...'I honestly wish I were dead'": Sappho, Poem 94. For a discussion, see Page, *Sappho and Alcaeus*, 75–83; Snyder, *Lesbian Desire*, 55–60; Johnson, *Sappho*, 84–87.

127 And just as Hera anoints herself: Homer, *Iliad* 14.153–92.

127 "...Sardis / ... often turning her thoughts to this": Sappho, Poem 96. Only the first part of the poem is given here. For commentary, see Snyder, *Lesbian Desire*, 45–55; Johnson, *Sappho*, 87–93.

128 "I loved you, Atthis, once long ago": Sappho, Poem 49.

128 "for you, Atthis ...": Sappho, Poem 8.

129 "shameful friendship": *Suda* S 107, in *Greek Lyric I: Sappho and*

Alcaeus, ed. David Campbell (Cambridge, MA: Harvard University Press, 2002), 4–7.

129   "But Atthis, it's become hateful": Sappho, Poem 131.

129   "What country girl bewitches your mind . . .": Sappho, Poem 57.

130   "The moon in its fullness appeared": Sappho, Poem 154.

CHAPTER SIX: THE GODDESS

133   "In the beginning there was Chaos": Hesiod, *Theogony* 116–22.

133   Ancient Greek religion: The best scholarly introduction to Greek religion is Walter Burkert, *Greek Religion* (Cambridge, MA: Harvard University Press, 1985). An excellent look at women in Greek religion is Joan Breton Connelly, *Portrait of a Priestess: Women and Ritual in Ancient Greece* (Princeton, NJ: Princeton University Press, 2007).

140   "I talked with you in a dream": Sappho, Poem 134.

140   ". . . you and my servant Love": Sappho, Poem 159.

141   "Come to me here from Crete": Sappho, Poem 2. For a discussion of the poem, see Denys Page, *Sappho and Alcaeus: An Introduction to the Study of Ancient Lesbian Poetry* (Oxford: Clarendon, 1965), 34–44; Anne Carson, *If Not, Winter: Fragments of Sappho* (New York: Vintage Books, 2002), 6–7, 358–59; Marguerite Johnson, *Sappho* (Bristol, England: Bristol Classical Press, 2007), 50–54; Anne L. Klinck, "Sappho's Company of Friends," *Hermes* 136 (2008): 17–18; Aaron Poochigian, *Sappho: Stung with Love: Poems and Fragments* (New York: Penguin, 2009), 4–5.

142   a powerful trance such as that: Homer, *Iliad* 14.359.

142   which overcomes an audience: Pindar, *Pythian* 1.12.

142   "The moon in its fullness appeared": Sappho, Poem 154.

144   "Come close to me, I pray": Sappho, Poem 17.

145   "The people of Lesbos founded": Alcaeus, Poem 129.

146   Alcaeus and a later ancient commentator: Alcaeus, Poem 130;

Scholiast on *Iliad* 9.129 (David Campbell, ed., *Greek Lyric I: Sappho and Alcaeus* [Cambridge, MA: Harvard University Press, 2002], 300–303). See also Jerome D. Quinn, "Cape Phokas, Lesbos: Site of an Archaic Sanctuary for Zeus, Hera and Dionysus?" *American Journal for Archaeology* 65, no. 4 (1961): 391–93.

146 **"'Delicate Adonis is dying, Cytherea'":** Sappho, Poem 140. Sappho also mourns Adonis in Poem 168.

CHAPTER SEVEN: UNYIELDING TIME

149 **"It's not by strength":** Cicero, *On Growing Old* 17.

149 **"Here lies Ennia Fructosa":** *Corpus Inscriptionum Latinarum* 8.2756.

150 **The Greeks had no concept of middle age:** Robert Garland, *The Greek Way of Life* (Ithaca, NY: Cornell University Press, 1990), 242–45. The whole of Garland's chapter "Elders and the Elderly" (pages 242–87) is an excellent introduction to old age in ancient Greece.

150 **"There was once a man of middle age":** Babrius, *Fable* 22.

151 **"A woman who leaves her house":** Hyperides frag. 205.

151 **Greek medical writers:** Aristotle, *History of Animals* 7.585b2–5; Aristotle, *Politics* 7.1335a9; Soranus, *Gynecology* 1.20.1, 26.3–5.

152 **"It is precious, this light the gods send":** Euripides, *Alcestis* 722.

152 **"O shining Odysseus":** Homer, *Odyssey* 11.488–91.

153 **"But when you die you will lie there":** Sappho, Poem 55.

155 **". . . beautiful gifts . . . children":** Sappho, Poem 58.

156 **Then, exactly eighty years later:** See the excellent essays on the rediscovery, text, translation, and interpretation of this poem in Ellen Greene and Marilyn B. Skinner, eds., *The New Sappho on Old Age: Textual and Philosophical Issues* (Washington, DC: Center for Hellenic Studies, 2009).

157 **This discovery was so startling:** M. L. West, "A New Sappho Poem," *Times Literary Supplement*, June 25, 2005.

158 **"a small masterpiece, simple, concise":** Ibid.

158　"Sappho is simply nothing less": "Sappho," *Saturday Review*, February 21, 1914, 228.

159　"It is not right in the house": Sappho, Poem 150.

EPILOGUE

161　"Someone, I say, will remember us": Sappho, Poem 147.

161　Sappho was certainly the first and greatest: For other female poets, see Jane McIntosh Snyder, *The Woman and the Lyre: Women Writers in Classical Greece and Rome* (Carbondale, IL: Southern Illinois University Press, 1989); Ellen Greene, ed., *Women Poets in Ancient Greece and Rome* (Norman: University of Oklahoma Press, 2005).

162　but we do have a paraphrase: Plutarch, *Moralia* 300cd.

162　In the next century, a woman named Corinna: Her dates are disputed, with some scholars claiming that Corinna lived in the third century BC.

162　She was reportedly a rival of Pindar: Pausanias 9.22; Aelian, *History* 13.25.

162　"I sing of the great deeds": Corinna frag. 664b.

163　"O friend, watch out": Praxilla frag. 750.

163　"O you who gaze in such beauty": Praxilla frag. 754.

163　When Argos was attacked by the Spartans: Pausanias 2.20.8. Modern scholars are skeptical of the veracity of this story, but it could well be true.

164　"This is the Lesbian honeycomb of Erinna": *Greek Anthology* 9.190.

165　"No bedchamber and sacred marriage rites for you": Ibid., 7.649.

165　"For her grasshopper, nightingale of the fields": Ibid., 7.190.

165　The town was unusual: Polybius, *Histories* 12.5.9.

165　"Nothing is sweeter than Eros": *Greek Anthology* 5.170.

166　"Stranger, if you sail to Mytilene": Ibid., 7.718.

166　"Come to the temple": Ibid., 9.332.

167　"At last love has come": Sulpicia, Poem 1.

168　the power of each generation: The best introductions to the afterlife of Sappho are Joan DeJean, *Fictions of Sappho: 1546–1937* (Chicago: University of Chicago Press, 1989); Ellen Greene, ed., *Re-reading Sappho: Reception and Transmission* (Berkeley: University of California Press, 1996); Yopie Prins, *Victorian Sappho* (Princeton, NJ: Princeton University Press, 1999); Margaret Reynolds, *The Sappho Companion* (New York: Palgrave, 2000); Marguerite Johnson, *Sappho* (Bristol, England: Bristol Classical Press, 2007), 19–40, 122–42.

168 **"Some people say there are nine Muses"**: According to Aelian, *Miscellaneous Histories* 12.9. The *Palatine Anthology* (9.506) allegedly reproduces the words of Plato in calling her the tenth muse. In Plato's genuine dialogue *Phaedrus* (235v), the philosopher does speak of "lovely Sappho" in the same breath as Anacreon.

168 **"Sappho, so goes the story"**: Menander frag. 258.

170 **". . . the love / of the Aeolian girl breathes still"**: Horace, *Ode* 4.9.

171 **"So if the fire still burns in your breast"**: Ovid, *Tristia* 3.7.

171 **"The stars around the beautiful moon"**: Sappho, Poem 34.

172 **"The passage of time has destroyed Sappho"**: Tzetzes, *On the Meters of Pindar* 20–22.

THE POEMS OF SAPPHO

174 **Poem 1:** Dionysius of Halicarnassus, *On the Arrangement of Words* 173–79; Oxyrhynchus papyrus 2288, http://www.papyrology .ox.ac.uk/POxy.

This poem is preserved by Dionysius of Halicarnassus, who wrote a book on literary style at the time of the Roman emperor Augustus. He quotes and praises this prayer of Sappho as "polished and exuberant," with the words skillfully woven together. Parts of the poem are also preserved in a second-century-AD Oxyrhynchus papyrus fragment.

The first word of the poem in Greek presents a problem. The

adjective *poikilothron* ("on a dazzling/ornate throne") also appears in some early manuscripts as *poikilophron* ("wily-minded"). The former is better attested in the manuscript tradition, but an argument can be made for either as the original. Which word editors and translators choose depends on what they think Sappho is saying. Is she sitting on her beautiful throne in the heavens (an image often found of the gods in ancient Greek art and literature), or does she want to highlight from the first word that Aphrodite is a crafty goddess?

In the second stanza, *chrusion* ("golden") could modify either the house of Zeus or Aphrodite's chariot in the following stanza. A punctuation mark in the papyrus fragment suggests the house is the best choice, but once again, either would work.

175 **Poem 2:** Florence ostracon (*Papyri Greci e Latini* 1300); Hermogenes, *On Kinds of Style* 2.4; Athenaeus, *Learned Diners* 11.463e.

Unique among the poems of Sappho, these verses are preserved primarily on a piece of broken pottery (an *ostracon*), measuring only a few inches across, from the third century BC. It was first published just before World War II and is now housed in the Laurentian Library Biblioteca Medicea Laurenziana in Florence, Italy. The faded Greek letters are difficult to read in several places, inviting many attempts over the years to fill in the gaps.

A few lines of the second and fourth stanzas with slight variants also survive in quotations by two later ancient authors, Hermogenes and Athenaeus.

At the top of the potsherd, a few letters are visible before the start of the poem. They seem to read *anothen katiou*—perhaps "coming down from heaven"—but the meaning is uncertain, as is the fact of whether those words belong with this poem.

The third stanza presents several problems, both because it's difficult to read what is written on the potsherd and because part of the third line and all of the last line are omitted. Blossoming spring flowers and gentle breezes seem fairly certain, but what Sappho intended next is unknown. The same is true for a missing word from the middle of the first line of the final stanza.

176   **Poem 3:** Berlin parchment 5006; Oxyrhynchus papyrus 424.

Lines 1–10 of this poem are preserved on a seventh-century-AD parchment housed in Berlin. Lines 6–15 are found on a fragmentary third-century-AD papyrus from Oxyrhynchus, Egypt.

177   **Poem 4:** Berlin parchment 5006.

These fragmentary verses are from the same seventh-century-AD parchment as the first few lines of Poem 3. The beginning of the final word (. . . *chroistheis*) is missing. I translate it as "joined together," though it could also mean "stained" or "ingrained."

177   **Poem 5:** Oxyrhynchus papyrus 7.

This was the first of Sappho's poems discovered by Grenfell and Hunt at Oxyrhynchus and published in 1898.

In some previous editions of Sappho, the poem was assumed to begin with an invocation of Cypris, the goddess Aphrodite, so called because she was born on the shores of the island of Cyprus, but this may not be the case. The Nereids were divine sea nymphs who, if so inclined, guided voyagers safely home.

The subject of the poem is Sappho's wayward brother Charaxus, who traveled to Egypt and fell in love there with a notorious prostitute named Doricha, bringing great shame on the family in Sappho's eyes. The final word of the poem is Greek *kakan*, a feminine singular, so the line could also be translated as ". . . putting aside the evil *woman*."

178   **Poem 6:** Oxyrhynchus papyrus 2289, frag. 1.

In a later fragment (Poem 157) Sappho uses the term "Lady Dawn," whose morning rays another Greek lyric poet (Bacchylides 5.40) describes as "golden armed." The final word of the poem, *kara*, could also be translated as "doom" or "disgrace."

178   **Poem 7:** Oxyrhynchus papyrus 2289, frag. 2.

Though the beginning of the first word is missing, it is likely the name of the Egyptian prostitute Doricha, loved by Sappho's brother Charaxus (see Poems 5 and 15).

179   **Poem 8:** Oxyrhynchus papyrus 2289, frag. 3.

Atthis, a companion of Sappho, is also mentioned in Poems 49, 96, and 131, as well as by the ancient orator Maximus of Tyre (*Orations* 18.9). The Byzantine *Suda* encyclopedia (S 107) says Sappho's relationship with Atthis and two other women earned her a reputation for "shameful love."

179 **Poem 9:** Oxyrhynchus papyrus 2289, frag. 4.

In Greek mythology, Hera is the wife of Zeus and a goddess especially worshipped by the women of Lesbos (see Poem 17).

179 **Poem 12:** Oxyrhynchus papyrus 2289, frag. 8.

179 **Poem 15:** Oxyrhynchus papyrus 1231, frag. 1.

Similar to Poem 5, this prayer by Sappho to the goddess Aphrodite (Cypris) is for the safe return of her wayward brother Charaxus from the arms of the Egyptian prostitute Doricha.

180 **Poem 16:** Oxyrhynchus papyri 1231, frag. 1; 2166, frag. 2; *Papiri Greci e Latini* 123, 1–2.

The first stanza uses a literary device called a *priamel*, in which several items are listed, followed by one preferred by the author.

Sappho uses the Greek plural pronoun *hoi* in the first stanza, which can refer to people in general, regardless of gender ("Some say . . ."). But since *hoi* is also the masculine form, the verses could be translated to give the stanza a little more bite ("Some *men* say . . .").

Helen, wife of Menelaus, left her husband and young daughter Hermione to run away to Troy with Paris, prince of that city, setting in motion the Trojan War.

This is the only surviving poem of Sappho that mentions Anactoria, but the tradition that she was loved by Sappho is echoed in Ovid (*Heroides* 15) and Maximus of Tyre (*Orations* 18.9).

The wealthy kingdom of Lydia in western Asia Minor is featured several times in Sappho's poetry as the producer of luxury goods, but as she notes here, it was also well known for its formidable military power.

181 **Poem 17:** *Papiri Greci e Latini* 123, 3–12; Oxyrhynchus papyri 1231, frag. 1; 2166, frag. 3; 2289, frag. 9.

The sons of Atreus are the brothers Agamemnon and Menelaus,

two kings who fought on the Greek side in the war against Troy. In a story in Homer's *Odyssey* (3.133ff), the brothers quarreled after Troy fell and sailed home separately, Menelaus stopping at Lesbos to pray to Zeus. Here we have an alternate version probably told on Sappho's island in which the brothers arrived together and prayed not only to Zeus, but to his wife Hera and to Dionysus (son of Thyone), rather than to Semele as in most versions.

According to Sappho's contemporary Alcaeus (Poem 129), there was a shrine of Hera on Lesbos at which Zeus and Dionysus were also worshipped. An annual beauty contest and dances for the women of Lesbos were reportedly held at the shrine.

182   **Poem 18:** Oxyrhynchus papyrus 1231, frag. 1.

The first word of the poem (*pan*, translated here as "all") could also be read as *Pan*, the Greek god of shepherds and wild places.

182   **Poem 19:** Oxyrhynchus papyrus 1231, frag. 2.

The participles "waiting," "having," and "going" are all feminine singular and could also be translated as "her waiting," and so on.

182   **Poem 20:** Oxyrhynchus papyrus 1231, frag. 9.

Like Poem 5, this may be a prayer for safe return from a sea voyage.

183   **Poem 21:** Oxyrhynchus papyrus 1231, frag. 10.

These fragmentary verses appear similar in theme to Sappho's newly restored Poem 58 on old age. I follow Anne Carson (*If Not, Winter: Fragments of Sappho* [New York: Vintage Books, 2002], 39) in reading the adjective *iokolpon* (which also appears in Sappho Poems 30 and 103) as "with violets in her lap," though it could also mean something like "violet-robed" or "wearing a belt of violets."

184   **Poem 22:** Oxyrhynchus papyrus 1231, frags. 12, 15.

Gongyla is named in the Byzantine *Suda* encyclopedia as a pupil of Sappho from Colophon in western Asia Minor. She also appears in Poems 95 and 213A, as well as in a second-century-AD papyrus commentary on lyric poetry (Oxyrhynchus papyrus 2637). Another papyrus commentary (Oxyrhynchus papyrus 2293) calls Gongyla a "yoke-mate" of Sappho's rival Gorgo. The postponed adjective "beautiful" at the beginning of the third stanza probably refers to Gongyla.

A fragment of a poem attributed to Sappho's contemporary Alcaeus (261b) mentions the dancing of "lovely Abanthis."

184 **Poem 23:** Oxyrhynchus papyrus 1231, frag. 14.

Hermione was the daughter of Helen of Troy and the Spartan king Menelaus (see Sappho Poem 16). Helen, considered the most beautiful woman in the world, was traditionally described as having golden-blond hair.

185 **Poem 24:** Oxyrhynchus papyri 1231, frags. 13, 17, 22, 25; 2166(a), frag. 7a.

186 **Poem 25:** Oxyrhynchus papyrus 1231, frag. 18.

186 **Poem 26:** Oxyrhynchus papyrus 1231, frag. 16.

See *The Cypris Poem*, page 238.

186 **Poem 27:** Oxyrhynchus papyri 1231, frags. 50–54; 2166(a), frag. 5.

187 **Poem 29:** Oxyrhynchus papyri 1231, frag. 11, for Poem 29B; 1231, frag. 19, and 2166(a), frag. 4b for Poem 29C; 2166(a), frag. 1, for Poem 29H.

The numerous fragments of Poem 29 yield only a few words that can be reconstructed with any confidence.

"Lady" is from the Greek word *Potnia*, found elsewhere in Sappho's poetry (Poems 6, 17) as a title for a goddess.

The name Gorgo—not a certain reading in this papyrus—is that of a rival of Sappho mentioned by Maximus of Tyre (*Orations* 18.9) and in Sappho's Poems 103Aa and 144.

Gyrinno, or Gyrinna, appears as a companion of Sappho also in Maximus of Tyre (*Orations* 18.9), in Sappho's Poem 82A, and in a second-century-AD commentary (Oxyrhynchus papyrus 2293).

188 **Poem 30:** Oxyrhynchus papyri 1231, frag. 56; 2166(a), frag. 6a.

The clear-voiced singer is almost certainly a nightingale.

188 **Poem 31:** Longinus, *On the Sublime* 10.

This is one of the most celebrated poems of Sappho, quoted and discussed by an author called Longinus who wrote on literary style in the first century AD. The first-century-BC Roman poet Catullus wrote a famous Latin adaptation of this poem (Catullus, Poem 51).

The final sentence of the quotation includes what is probably the beginning of the final stanza of the poem. The phrase "must be endured" could also mean "must be dared."

189 **Poem 32:** Apollonius Dyscolus, *Pronouns* 144a.

A brief quotation found in the second-century-AD grammarian Apollonius Dyscolus, who lived and worked in Alexandria, Egypt. The line may refer to the muses.

189 **Poem 33:** Apollonius Dyscolus, *Syntax* 3.247.

190 **Poem 34:** Eustathius on Homer, *Iliad* 8.555.

The twelfth-century-AD Byzantine churchman Eustathius wrote commentaries on classical literature before devoting himself entirely to religious affairs. In his commentary on a passage from the *Iliad*, he records this stanza of Sappho.

The fourth-century-AD Roman emperor Julian also mentions it in one of his letters (*Epistle* 194): "Sappho . . . says the moon is silver and because of this hides the other stars from view." Sappho uses a similar image in Poem 96.

190 **Poem 35:** Strabo 1.2.33.

The first-century-BC Greek geographer Strabo quotes this line, the context of which is unknown. Cyprus is the island where Aphrodite was born, specifically at Paphos on the southwestern coast. Panormus is modern-day Palermo in Sicily, the island to which Sappho was exiled.

190 **Poem 36:** *Etymologicum gudianum* 294.40.

Quoted in a Byzantine dictionary of the 11th century AD.

190 **Poem 37:** *Etymologicum genuinum* 213.

The ninth- or tenth-century-AD Byzantine dictionary quoting this first line says that writers in the Aeolian dialect of Greek used the word *stalagmon* ("dripping"—root of English "stalagmite") to describe pain, because it drips and flows.

191 **Poem 38:** Apollonius Dyscolus, *Pronouns* 127a.

The grammarian Apollonius Dyscolus identifies these words as coming from the first book of Sappho's collected poetry. The

Greek verb *optao* ("scorch, burn") is often used metaphorically in love poetry.

191 **Poem 39:** Ancient commentator on Aristophanes, *Peace* 1174.

191 **Poem 40:** Apollonius Dyscolus, *Pronouns* 104c.

191 **Poem 41:** Ibid., 124c.

191 **Poem 42:** Ancient commentator on Pindar, *Pythian* 1.10.

The commentator says that Sappho is referring to pigeons.

192 **Poem 43:** Oxyrhynchus papyrus 1232, frag. 1.

192 **Poem 44:** Oxyrhynchus papyri 1232, frags. 1–2; 2076.

This is one of the longest of Sappho's poems discovered in modern times. Its subject, the arrival at Troy of prince Hector and his bride Andromache, is an episode not found in Homer's *Iliad*. These verses differ from much of Sappho's poetry by their use of a longer metrical line similar to that found in an epic. The vocabulary, grammar, and syntax here is also reminiscent of Homer, but the setting and details draw on the culture of the Lesbos of Sappho's own time.

Andromache was the daughter of the king of Thebe, a city near Troy. The Placia river was near Thebe. Paean is a name for the god Apollo.

193 **Poem 44Aa/Ab:** Fouad papyrus 239.

This second- or third-century-AD papyrus, in two columns containing parts of two poems, was published in 1952 and assigned tentatively to Alcaeus, Sappho's contemporary from Lesbos. Subsequently, other scholars have argued that the fragments belong to Sappho.

Phoebus is the god Apollo, son of Leto, the daughter of the Titan Coeus, fathered by Zeus, the son of Cronus. Artemis is his sister by the same parents.

194 **Poem 45:** Apollonius Dyscolus, *Pronouns* 119b.

194 **Poem 46:** Herodian, *On Anomalous Words* 2.945.

The second-century-AD grammarian Herodian quotes these lines of Sappho because they contain the unusual word *tule* ("cushion").

194　**Poem 47:** Maximus of Tyre, *Orations* 18.9.

　　　The second-century-AD orator Maximus quotes this line comparing the effect of love (*eros*) on Sappho and the Athenian philosopher Socrates.

195　**Poem 48:** Julian, *Epistle* 183.

195　**Poem 49:** Hephaestion, *Handbook of Meters* 7.7; Plutarch, *Dialogue on Love* 751d; Terentianus Maurus 2154–55.

　　　The first line is given as an example of the fourteen-syllable meter of Sappho by the second-century-AD scholar Hephaestion, while the second line (probably from a different poem) is quoted by the writer Plutarch a century earlier with the comment that Sappho is addressing a girl too young to marry. The grammarian Terentianus Maurus, a few decades after Hephaestion, quotes the lines together.

　　　Atthis is also mentioned in Poems 8, 96, and 131, as well as in several ancient authors and commentaries.

195　**Poem 50:** Galen, *Exhortation to Learning* 8.16.

　　　The second-century-AD physician and philosopher Galen quotes these lines after making the following comment: "Since we know that the prime of youth is like the flowers of spring and gives brief pleasure, it is better to commend the woman of Lesbos when she says . . ."

195　**Poem 51:** Chrysippus, *On Negatives* 23.

195　**Poem 52:** Herodian, *On Anomalous Words* 2.912.

196　**Poem 53:** Ancient commentator on Theocritus 28.

196　**Poem 54:** Pollux, *Vocabulary* 10.124.

　　　The second-century-AD scholar Pollux quotes this line, saying Sappho is speaking of the god Eros (Love) when she is the first writer to use the Greek word *chlamus*, a type of short cloak.

196　**Poem 55:** Stobaeus, *Anthology* 3.4.12.

　　　The fifth-century-AD anthologizer Stobaeus says that Sappho wrote these lines to an uneducated woman. Three centuries earlier, Plutarch says in one passage (*Advice to Bride and Groom* 145f–146a) that the verses are addressed to a wealthy woman, and in another

(*Table Talk* 646e–f), that they are about an uncultured, ignorant woman.

Pieria in northern Greece is the birthplace of the muses.

196 **Poem 56:** Chrysippus, *On Negatives* 13.

197 **Poem 57:** Athenaeus, *Learned Diners* 21b–c; Maximus of Tyre, *Orations* 18.9.

Athenaeus says that Sappho is deriding her rival Andromeda, who also appears in Poem 131.

197 **Poem 58:** Oxyrhynchus papyrus 1787, frags. 1–2; Cologne papyri 21351, 21376. See Dirk Obbink, "Sappho Fragments 58–59: Text, Apparatus Criticus, and Translation," in *The New Sappho on Old Age: Textual and Philosophical Issues*, eds. Ellen Greene and Marilyn B. Skinner (Washington, DC: Center for Hellenic Studies, 2009), 7–16.

198 **Poem 59:** Oxyrhynchus papyrus 1787, frag. 2.

198 **Poem 60:** Ibid., frag. 44.

199 **Poem 61:** Ibid., frag. 3.

199 **Poem 62:** Ibid.

199 **Poem 63:** Ibid.

200 **Poem 64A:** Ibid., frag. 17.

200 **Poem 65:** Ibid., frag. 4.

In this poem, Aphrodite may be promising glory to Sappho even after death beyond the underworld river of Acheron.

201 **Poem 67A:** Oxyrhynchus papyrus 1787, frag. 5.

201 **Poem 67B:** Ibid., frag. 18.

201 **Poem 68A:** Ibid., frag. 7.

Andromeda was a rival of Sappho; Megara was Sappho's companion. The sons of Tyndareus are Castor and Pollux, brothers of Helen of Troy.

202 **Poem 68B:** Oxyrhynchus papyrus 1787, frag. 19.

202 **Poem 69:** Ibid., frag. 32.

202 **Poem 70:** Ibid., frag. 13.

The Greek word for "harmony" could also be a woman's name, "Harmonia."

203 Poem 71: Oxyrhynchus papyri 1787, frag. 6; Bernard Grenfell and Arthur Hunt, eds., *The Oxyrhynchus Papyri* (London: Egypt Exploration Fund, 1898), 21:135.

The house of Penthilus was a powerful family of Lesbos into which Pittacus—tyrant of Lesbos and enemy of Sappho's family—married.

203 Poem 73A: Oxyrhynchus papyrus 1787, frag. 11.

204 Poem 74A–C: Ibid., frag. 16.

204 Poem 76: Ibid., frag. 12.

204 Poem 78: Ibid., frag. 10.

205 Poem 80: Ibid., frag. 15.

205 Poem 81: Ibid., frag. 33; Athenaeus, *Learned Diners* 15.674e.

The first two lines are from the papyrus fragment; the remainder is quoted by Athenaeus.

205 Poem 82A: Hephaestion, *Handbook of Meters* 11.5.

Gyrinno, or Gyrinna, was a companion of Sappho (see Poem 29).

205 Poem 82A/B: Oxyrhynchus papyrus 1787, frag. 34.

The Greek word *eumorphotera* ("more finely shaped") is used in both of these poems.

206 Poem 83: Ibid., frag. 36.

206 Poem 84: Ibid., frags. 37, 41.

206 Poem 85B: Ibid., frag. 38.

207 Poem 86: Oxyrhynchus papyrus 1787 = 2166(d), frag. 1.

The aegis was a divine breastplate associated in Homer primarily with Zeus, and then later with Athena, but not with Cytherea, another name for Aphrodite.

207 Poem 87A: Oxyrhynchus papyrus 1787, frag. 14.

207 Poem 87B: Ibid., frag. 30.

207 Poem 87C: Ibid., frag. 43.

208 Poem 87D: Oxyrhynchus papyrus 2166(d), frag. 3.

208 Poem 87E: Ibid., frag. 6.

208 Poem 87F: Ibid., frag. 7.

208 Poem 88AB: Oxyrhynchus papyrus 2290.

209 Poem 91: Hephaestion, *Handbook on Meters* 11.5.

209 Poem 92: Berlin parchment 9722, folio 1.

210 Poem 93: Ibid., folio 3.

210 Poem 94: Ibid., folio 2.

Since the beginning of the poem is lost, we can't be sure if the one wishing she were dead is Sappho or the woman who is leaving her, though the latter is more likely.

211 Poem 95: Berlin parchment 9722, folio 4.

Gongyla was a pupil of Sappho (Poem 22). The master the poet addresses may be the god Hermes, who led departed souls to the river Acheron (see Poem 65) in the land of the dead. In Homer's *Odyssey* (Book 9), Odysseus and his men barely escape from a land where the inhabitants eat the lotus flower and forget all pain.

212 Poem 96: Berlin parchment 9722, folio 5.

A young woman, deeply attached to Atthis, has departed from Sappho's circle and gone to Sardis, the chief city of Lydia across the sea in Asia Minor. The Geraesteum is probably the temple of the sea god Poseidon on the island of Euboea.

213 Poem 97: Berlin parchment 9722, folio 5.

214 Poem 98A/B: Copenhagen papyrus 301; Milan papyrus 32.

These poems seem to be set at a time when Sappho and her family are in exile and out of power in Mytilene, the ruling city of Lesbos. Sappho tells her daughter, Cleis, that she regretfully can't provide her with a fashionable headband, such as girls wore when Sappho's own mother was young. This is because the Cleanactidae, the family of Cleanax and the enemies of Sappho's family, are in power.

215 Poem 100: Pollux, *Vocabulary* 7.73.

215 Poem 101: Athenaeus, *Learned Diners* 9.410e.

Phocaea was a Greek city known for seafaring and trade on the coast of Asia Minor just south of Lesbos. Athenaeus says that Sappho is addressing Aphrodite and meant "hand cloths" as adornments for the head.

215 Poem 102: Hephaestion, *Handbook on Meters* 10.5.

216 **Poem 103:** Oxyrhynchus papyrus 2294.

The heading of the papyrus says that this is a list of the first lines of ten poems.

216 **Poem 103Aa/Ab:** Cairo papyrus 7.

217 **Poem 103B:** Oxyrhynchus papyrus 2308.

217 **Poem 103Ca/Cb:** Oxyrhynchus papyrus 2357, frags. 1, 4.

218 **Poem 104A:** Demetrius, *On Style* 141.

218 **Poem 104B:** Himerius, *Orations* 46.8.

218 **Poem 105A:** Syrianus on Hermogenes, *On Kinds of Style* 1.1.

Himerius, in his *Orations* (9.16), says that Sappho compares a girl to an apple.

218 **Poem 105B:** Demetrius, *On Style* 106.

219 **Poem 106:** Ibid., 146.

Demetrius says Sappho is speaking of an outstanding man. The superiority of Lesbian singers became proverbial.

219 **Poem 107:** Apollonius Dyscolus, *Conjunctions* 490.

219 **Poem 108:** Himerius, *Orations* 9.19.

219 **Poem 109:** Ancient commentary on Homer, *Iliad* 1.528.

219 **Poem 110:** Hephaestion, *Handbook on Meters* 7.6.

The ancient commentator Pollux, *Vocabulary* (3.42) says the doorkeeper kept the bride's friends from coming to her rescue—part of the wedding night ritual. Demetrius (*On Style* 167) says Sappho was poking fun at the rustic bridegroom and his doorkeeper by using deliberately nonpoetic language.

220 **Poem 111:** Hephaestion, *On Poems* 7.1.

This bawdy wedding song compares the eager bridegroom and his huge erection to the war god Ares. The bridegroom's penis is so huge that the carpenters allegedly have to raise up the roof for him to enter the bridal chamber. Hymenaeus was a god of marriage.

J. D. Salinger borrowed from the poem for the title of his 1955 novella *Raise High the Roof Beam, Carpenters*.

220 **Poem 112:** Hephaestion, *Handbook on Meters* 15.26.

The first part of this wedding song is addressed to the groom, the latter to the bride.

220 **Poem 113:** Dionysius of Halicarnassus, *On Literary Composition* 25.

221 **Poem 114:** Demetrius, *On Style* 140.

Demetrius explains that repetition is skillfully used in this poem, with the first line spoken by a bride, the second by her virginity.

221 **Poem 115:** Hephaestion, *Handbook on Meters* 7.6.

221 **Poem 116:** Servius on Virgil, *Georgics* 1.31.

221 **Poem 117:** Hephaestion, *Handbook on Meters* 4.2.

221 **Poem 117A:** Hesychius, *Lexicon "xoanon."*

222 **Poem 118:** Hermogenes, *On Kinds of Style* 2.4.

Hermogenes says that Sappho speaks to her lyre and the lyre answers, but its response has been lost.

222 **Poem 119:** Ancient commentator on Aristophanes, *Plutus* 729.

222 **Poem 120:** *Etymologicum magnum* 2.43.

222 **Poem 121:** Stobaeus, *Anthology* 4.22.

222 **Poem 122:** Athenaeus, *Learned Diners* 12.554b.

Athenaeus says Sappho wrote this about Persephone, the maiden daughter of the goddess Demeter, who was kidnapped by Hades to be his bride in the underworld.

223 **Poem 123:** Ammonius, *On Similar but Different Words* 75.

223 **Poem 124:** Hephaestion, *Handbook on Meters* 15.4.

Calliope was the muse of lyric poetry.

223 **Poem 125:** Ancient commentator on Aristophanes, *Thesmophoriazusae* 401.

The commentator says it was the custom, as described by Sappho, of young people and those in love to weave garlands.

223 **Poem 126:** *Etymologicum genuinum* 22.

223 **Poem 127:** Hephaestion, *Handbook on Meters* 15.25.

224 **Poem 128:** Ibid., 9.2.

224 **Poem 129A/B:** Apollonius Dyscolus, *Pronouns* 1.66.

224 **Poem 130:** Hephaestion, *Handbook on Meters* 7.7.

224 **Poem 131:** Ibid.

Atthis was Sappho's companion; Andromeda was Sappho's rival.

225 Poem 132: Hephaestion, *Handbook on Meters* 15.18.

Cleis was Sappho's daughter (Poem 98B).

225 Poem 133A/B: Hephaestion, *Handbook on Meters* 14.7.

The word "revenge" can also mean "exchange" or "recompense."

225 Poem 134: Hephaestion, *Handbook on Meters* 12.4.

"Cyprus-born" refers to the goddess Aphrodite.

225 Poem 135: Hephaestion, *Handbook on Meters* 12.2.

Pandion's daughter is Procne, child of the king of Athens, who was changed into a swallow. Sappho mentions Irana in Poem 91 as well.

226 Poem 136: Ancient commentator on Sophocles, *Electra* 149.

226 Poem 137: Aristotle, *Rhetoric* 1367a.

Aristotle says the first two lines are spoken by Alcaeus, Sappho's contemporary poet in Lesbos, but it could well be, as a later commentator claims, that Sappho wrote both sides of the dialogue.

226 Poem 138: Athenaeus, *Learned Diners* 13.564d.

The translation of the first line is uncertain, but Athenaeus says that Sappho is addressing a man much admired for his form and handsomeness. It may be that she is being sarcastic.

226 Poem 139: Oxyrhynchus papyrus 1356, folio 4.

A fragment of uncertain meaning, but the author, Philo, says that it is better advice about the gods than a missing passage just before this one.

227 Poem 140: Hephaestion, *Handbook on Meters* 10.4.

This is one of the earliest references in Greek literature to the cult of Adonis, which spread west from Syria to the Aegean world. In mythology, Adonis was a lover of Aphrodite (Cytherea) but was killed by a wild boar and mourned by the goddess and her followers. Pausanias 9.29.8 says that Sappho sang of Adonis.

227 Poem 141: Athenaeus, *Learned Diners* 10.425d.

Ambrosia (literally "deathlessness") was the food of the gods. Athenaeus quotes these lines to show that Hermes was a wine pourer for the gods. The setting may be the wedding of the goddess Thetis to the mortal Peleus, father of Achilles.

227 **Poem 142:** Athenaeus, *Learned Diners* 13.571d.

Leto was a goddess and the mother of Apollo and Artemis by Zeus. Niobe was a mortal queen who boasted that she had more and better children than Leto. Apollo and Artemis killed all of her offspring as punishment.

Given the rivalry of the two mothers, this line claiming they were companions seems odd. The Greek term *(h)etairai* was often used in the centuries after Sappho for very expensive and well-trained prostitutes, but Athenaeus reports that it continued to be used for dear and intimate friends.

227 **Poem 143:** Athenaeus, *Learned Diners* 2.54f.

228 **Poem 144:** Herodian, *On the Declension of Nouns.*

Gorgo was a rival of Sappho.

228 **Poem 145:** Ancient commentator on Apollonius of Rhodes 1.1123.

The word *cherados* refers to small stones such as gravel. The line is likely proverbial. Sappho's contemporary Alcaeus (Poem 344) also speaks of it:

> *I know this for certain, that if a man moves gravel—such a*
> *tricky stone to work—he'll end up with a headache.*

228 **Poem 146:** Tryphon, *Figures of Speech* 25.

Quoted by the first-century-BC grammarian Tryphon, this line is a proverb that the ancient scholar Diogenian (*Proverbs* 6.58) says is used of those who are not willing to take the bad with the good.

228 **Poem 147:** Dio Chrysostom, *Discourses* 37.47.

228 **Poem 148:** Ancient commentator on Pindar, *Ode* 2.96.

229 **Poem 149:** Apollonius Dyscolus, *Pronouns* 126b.

229 **Poem 150:** Maximus of Tyre, *Orations* 18.9.

Maximus says that Socrates was angry at his wife, Xanthippe, for lamenting when he was dying, while Sappho likewise rebuked her daughter with these lines.

229 **Poem 151:** *Etymologicum genuinum* 19 (*Etymologicum magnum* 117.14ss.)

229 **Poem 152:** Ancient commentator on Apollonius of Rhodes 1.726.

229 **Poem 153:** Atilius Fortunatianus 6.301.

230 Poem 154: Hephaestion, *Handbook of Meters* 11.2.

230 Poem 155: Maximus of Tyre, *Orations* 18.9d.

Maximus says that both Socrates and Sappho used irony like this phrase in addressing their opponents. This line of Sappho could be translated several ways, including: "I wish the daughter of the house of Polyanax a fond farewell."

230 Poem 156: Demetrius, *On Style* 162.

Demetrius quotes this line in reference to effective hyperbole, saying that the charm of such phrases lies in their impossibility. Earlier (*On Style* 127), he writes that "one of the most amazing features of the divine Sappho is that she uses with charming effect a tool that is difficult and hazardous."

230 Poem 157: *Etymologicum genuinum* (*Etymologicum magnum* 174.43ss).

230 Poem 158: Plutarch, *On Restraining Anger* 456.

Plutarch says that when one is angry, there is nothing more dignified than silence, and then he quotes this advice from Sappho.

231 Poem 159: Maximus of Tyre, *Orations* 18.9.

Maximus writes that Aphrodite says this to Sappho in one of her poems.

231 Poem 160: Athenaeus, *Learned Diners* 13.571d.

231 Poem 161: Bouriant papyrus 8.90ss.

231 Poem 162: Choeroboscus, *On the Canons of Theodosius* 1.193.

231 Poem 163: Julian, *Epistle* 193.

232 Poem 164: Apollonius Dyscolus, *Pronouns* 136b.

232 Poem 165: Ibid., 106a.

This may be an alternate beginning of Poem 31.

232 Poem 166: Athenaeus, *Learned Diners* 2.57d.

In a story of classical mythology with many variants, Zeus in the form of a swan had sex with the mortal woman Leda, who gave birth to an egg from which hatched Helen and Pollux.

232 Poem 167: Athenaeus, *Learned Diners* 2.57d.

232 Poem 168: Marius Plotius Sacerdos, *Art of Grammar* 6.516.

232 Poem 168A: Zenobius, *Proverbs* 3.3.

The ancient collector of proverbs Zenobius says that Gello was a girl who died young and was said by the people of Lesbos to haunt little children, for whose deaths she was blamed.

233 **Poem 168B:** Hephaestion, *Handbook of Meters* 11.5.

233 **Poem 168C:** Demetrius, *On Style* 164.

233 **Poem 169:** Ancient commentator on Homer, *Iliad* 14.241.

233 **Poem 169A:** Hesychius, *Lexicon* A 1621.

233 **Poem 170:** Strabo 13.1.68.

Aiga is the name (meaning "the goat") of a promontory on mainland Asia Minor across from Lesbos.

234 **Poem 171:** Photius, *Lexicon* 1.370.

The Byzantine scholar Photius says Sappho used the word *akakos* ("innocent") of someone who has no experience with evil, not of someone who has experienced evil and rejected it.

234 **Poem 172:** Maximus of Tyre, *Orations* 18.9.

Maximus says that Sappho is speaking of Love (Eros) when she says the god is both bittersweet and *algesidoron* ("pain-giver").

234 **Poem 173:** Choeroboscus, *On the Canons of Theodosius* 1.331.4.

234 **Poem 174:** Orion, *Lexicon* 3.12ss.

234 **Poem 175:** Apollonius Dyscolus, *Adverbs* 596.

234 **Poem 176:** Athenaeus, *Learned Diners* 4.182f.

Barbitos and *baromos* are two different spellings of a word for "lyre" used by Sappho.

235 **Poem 177:** Pollux, *Vocabulary* 7.49.

Pollux defines the word *beudos* used by Sappho as a "short, transparent dress."

235 **Poem 179:** Phrynichus, *Sophistic Preparation* 60, 14ss.

According to Phrynichus, Sappho uses the word *gruta* to describe a bag used by women for perfume and other items.

235 **Poem 180:** Hesychius, *Lexicon* E 1750.

Hesychius reports that "the Holder" is a name Sappho gives to Zeus.

235 **Poem 181:** Ancient commentator on Dionysius of Thrace 493.

235 **Poem 182:** Ancient commentator on Homer, *Iliad* 14.241.

235 **Poem 183:** Porphyry, *Homeric Questions* on *Iliad* 2.447.

Porphyry says that Alcaeus and Sappho used the adjective *katore* to describe a down-rushing wind.

236 **Poem 184:** Choeroboscus, *On the Canons of Theodosius* 1.270.

236 **Poem 185:** Philostratus, *Pictures* 2.1; Aristaenetus, *Love Letters* 1.10.

Philostratus describes "honey-voiced" as "Sappho's delightful epithet," and Aristaenetus characterizes it as "Sappho's most delightful word." The two grammarians list two slightly different adjectives: *meliphonoi* and *mellichophonoi*, respectively.

236 **Poem 186:** John of Alexandria, *Rules of Accentuation* 4.29.

This word could be the name of the sorceress from the tale of Jason and the Argonauts (*Medea*) or the feminine singular form of *medeis* (*medeia*, meaning "no one").

236 **Poem 187:** *Homeric Parsings* on *Iliad* 2.761.

236 **Poem 188:** Maximus of Tyre, *Orations* 18.9.

Maximus says that Socrates calls Eros (Love) a sophist, while Sappho prefers *muthoplokon* ("weaver of tales").

236 **Poem 189:** Phrynichus, *Attic Words and Phrases* 272.

In the Attic Greek of Athens, the word for "carbonate of soda" is *litron*, but in Sappho and elsewhere, it is *nitron*.

237 **Poem 190:** Ancient commentator on Homer, *Iliad* 3.219.

237 **Poem 191:** Pollux, *Vocabulary* 6.107.

Pollux reports that both Sappho and Alcaeus use this word.

237 **Poem 192:** Pollux, *Vocabulary* 6.98.

Specifically, golden cups with bottoms shaped like knucklebones.

237 **The Brothers Poem:** See Dirk Obbink, "Two New Poems by Sappho," *Zeitschrift für Papyrologie und Epigraphik*, 189 (2014).

238 **The Cypris Poem:** Ibid.

FURTHER READING

Bagnall, Roger S., ed. *The Oxford Handbook of Papyrology*. Oxford: Oxford University Press, 2009.

Barnard, Mary. *Sappho*. Berkeley: University of California Press, 1958.

Betz, Hans Dieter, ed. *The Greek Magical Papyri in Translation*. Chicago: University of Chicago Press, 1992.

Bowman, A. K., R. A. Coles, N. Gonis, D. Obbink, and P. J. Parsons, eds. *Oxyrhynchus: A City and Its Texts*. London: Egypt Exploration Society, 2007.

Budelmann, Felix, ed. *The Cambridge Companion to Greek Lyric*. Cambridge: Cambridge University Press, 2009.

Burkert, Walter. *Greek Religion*. Cambridge, MA: Harvard University Press, 1985.

Burn, A. R. *The Lyric Age of Greece*. London: Edward Arnold, 1978.

Burnett, Anne Pippin. *Three Archaic Poets: Archilochus, Alcaeus, Sappho*. Cambridge, MA: Harvard University Press, 1983.

Calame, Claude. *The Poetics of Eros in Ancient Greece*. Princeton, NJ: Princeton University Press, 1999.

Campbell, David A. *Greek Lyric I: Sappho and Alcaeus*. Cambridge, MA: Harvard University Press, 2002.

————. *Greek Lyric Poetry*. Bristol, England: Bristol Classical Press, 1990.

Carson, Anne. *Eros the Bittersweet*. Champaign, IL: Dalkey Archive Press, 2009.

————. *If Not, Winter: Fragments of Sappho*. New York: Vintage Books, 2002.

Connelly, Joan Breton. *Portrait of a Priestess: Women and Ritual in Ancient Greece*. Princeton, NJ: Princeton University Press, 2007.

Davidson, James. *The Greeks and Greek Love*. New York: Random House, 2007.

DeJean, Joan. *Fictions of Sappho: 1546–1937*. Chicago: University of Chicago Press, 1989.

Demand, Nancy. *Birth, Death, and Motherhood in Classical Greece*. Baltimore: Johns Hopkins University Press, 1994.

Dover, K. J. *Greek Homosexuality*. Cambridge, MA: Harvard University Press, 1989.

DuBois, Page. *Sappho Is Burning*. Chicago: University of Chicago Press, 1995.

Edgeworth, Robert J. "Sappho Fr. 31.14." *Acta Classica* 27 (1984): 121–24.

Ehrman, Bart, and Zlatko Plese, eds. *The Apocryphal Gospels*. Oxford: Oxford University Press, 2011.

Fantham, Elaine, Helen Peet Foley, Natalie Boymel Kampen, Sarah B. Pomeroy, and H. A. Shapiro, eds. *Women in the Classical World: Image and Text*. Oxford: Oxford University Press, 1994.

Ferrari, Franco. *Sappho's Gift: The Poet and Her Community*. Ann Arbor: Michigan Classical Press, 2010.

Gager, John G. *Curse Tablets and Binding Spells from the Ancient World.* Oxford: Oxford University Press, 1992.

Garland, Robert. *The Greek Way of Death.* Ithaca, NY: Cornell University Press, 2001.

———. *The Greek Way of Life.* Ithaca, NY: Cornell University Press, 1990.

Gerber, Douglas E., ed. *A Companion to the Greek Lyric Poets.* Leiden, Netherlands: Brill, 2011.

Golden, Mark. *Children and Childhood in Classical Athens.* Baltimore: Johns Hopkins University Press, 1990.

Green, Peter. *The Laughter of Aphrodite: A Novel about Sappho of Lesbos.* Berkeley: University of California Press, 1993.

Greene, Ellen, ed. *Reading Sappho: Contemporary Approaches.* Berkeley: University of California Press, 1996.

———, ed. *Re-reading Sappho: Reception and Transmission.* Berkeley: University of California Press, 1996.

———, ed. *Women Poets in Ancient Greece and Rome.* Norman: University of Oklahoma Press, 2005.

Greene, Ellen, and Marilyn B. Skinner, eds. *The New Sappho on Old Age: Textual and Philosophical Issues.* Washington, DC: Center for Hellenic Studies, 2009.

Grubbs, Judith Evans, and Tim Parkin, eds. *The Oxford Handbook of Childhood and Education in the Classical World.* Oxford: Oxford University Press, 2013.

Hall, Jonathan M. *A History of the Archaic Greek World: ca. 1200–479 BCE.* Malden, MA: Wiley-Blackwell, 2014.

Hubbard, Thomas K., ed. *Homosexuality in Greece and Rome: A Sourcebook of Basic Documents.* Berkeley: University of California Press, 2003.

Hutchinson, G. O. *Greek Lyric Poetry: A Commentary on Selected Larger Pieces.* Oxford: Oxford University Press, 2001.

Irwin, Eleanor. *Colour Terms in Greek Poetry.* Toronto: Hakkert, 1974.

Jeffery, L. H. *Archaic Greece: The City States c. 700–500 B.C.* London: Methuen, 1978.

Johnson, Marguerite. *Sappho.* Bristol, England: Bristol Classical Press, 2007.

Keuls, Eva C. *The Reign of the Phallus: Sexual Politics in Ancient Athens.* Berkeley: University of California Press, 1985.

Klinck, Anne L. "Sappho's Company of Friends." *Hermes* 136 (2008): 15–29.

Kraemer, Ross Shepard. *Her Share of the Blessings: Women's Religions among Pagans, Jews, and Christians in the Greco-Roman World.* Oxford: Oxford University Press, 1992.

Lefkowitz, Mary R. *The Lives of the Greek Poets.* Baltimore: Johns Hopkins University Press, 2012.

Lefkowitz, Mary R., and Maureen B. Fant, eds. *Women's Life in Greece and Rome: A Sourcebook in Translation.* Baltimore: Johns Hopkins University Press, 1992.

Lobel, Edgar, and Denys Page. *Poetarum Lesbiorum Fragmenta.* Oxford: Clarendon, 1968.

Lombardo, Stanley. *Sappho: Poems and Fragments.* Indianapolis, IN: Hackett, 2002.

Luck, Georg. *Arcana Mundi: Magic and the Occult in the Greek and Roman Worlds.* Baltimore: Johns Hopkins University Press, 2006.

MacLachlan, Bonnie. *Women in Ancient Greece: A Sourcebook.* London: Continuum, 2012.

Meador, Betty De Shong. *Inanna: Lady of the Largest Heart.* Austin: University of Texas Press, 2000.

Neils, Jenifer. *Women in the Ancient World.* Los Angeles: J. Paul Getty Museum, 2011.

Neils, Jenifer, and John H. Oakley, eds. *Coming of Age in Ancient Greece.* New Haven, CT: Yale University Press, 2003.

Obbink, Dirk. "Provenance, Authenticity, and Text of the New Sappho Papyri." Paper presented at Society for Classical Studies Panel: New Fragments of Sappho, New Orleans, January 9, 2015.

Page, Denys. *Sappho and Alcaeus: An Introduction to the Study of Ancient Lesbian Poetry.* Oxford: Clarendon, 1965.

Parsons, Peter. *City of the Sharp-Nosed Fish.* London: Phoenix, 2007.

Petropoulos, J. C. B. "Sappho the Sorceress—Another Look at Fr. 1." *Zeitschrift für Papyrologie und Epigraphik* 97 (1993): 43–56.

Plant, I. M., ed. *Women Writers of Ancient Greece and Rome: An Anthology.* Norman: University of Oklahoma Press, 2004.

Pomeroy, Sarah B. *Spartan Women.* Oxford: Oxford University Press, 2002.

Poochigian, Aaron. *Sappho: Stung with Love: Poems and Fragments.* New York: Penguin, 2009.

Powell, Jim. *The Poetry of Sappho.* Oxford: Oxford University Press, 2007.

Prins, Yopie. *Victorian Sappho.* Princeton, NJ: Princeton University Press, 1999.

Quinn, Jerome D. "Cape Phokas, Lesbos: Site of an Archaic Sanctuary for Zeus, Hera and Dionysus?" *American Journal for Archaeology* 65, no. 4 (1961): 391–93.

Rayor, Diane J. *Sappho's Lyre: Archaic Lyric and Women Poets of Ancient Greece.* Berkeley: University of California Press, 1991.

Rayor, Diane J., and André Lardinois. *Sappho: A New Translation of the Complete Works.* Cambridge: Cambridge University Press, 2014.

Reynolds, Margaret. *The Sappho Companion.* New York: Palgrave, 2000.

Rhodes, P. J., and Robin Osborne, eds. *Greek Historical Inscriptions 404–323 BC.* Oxford: Oxford University Press, 2007.

Schaus, Gerald P. "Archaic Imported Fine Wares from the Acropolis, Mytilene" *Hesperia* 61, no. 3 (1992): 355–74.

Segal, Charles. "Eros and Incantation: Sappho and Oral Poetry." In *Reading Sappho: Contemporary Approaches*, edited by Ellen Greene, 58–75. Berkeley: University of California Press, 1996.

Skinner, Marilyn B. *Sexuality in Greek and Roman Culture.* Malden, MA: Wiley-Blackwell, 2014.

Snodgrass, Anthony. *Archaic Greece: The Age of Experiment.* Berkeley: University of California Press, 1981.

Snyder, Jane McIntosh. *Lesbian Desire in the Lyrics of Sappho.* New York: Columbia University Press, 1997.

———. *The Woman and the Lyre: Women Writers in Classical Greece and Rome.* Carbondale, IL: Southern Illinois University Press, 1989.

Spencer, Nigel. "Early Lesbos between East and West: A 'Grey Area' of Aegean Archaeology." *Annual of the British School at Athens* 90 (1995): 269–306.

Vivante, Bella. *Daughters of Gaia: Women in the Ancient Mediterranean World.* Norman: University of Oklahoma Press, 2008.

Voigt, Eva-Maria, ed. *Sappho et Alcaeus: Fragmenta.* Amsterdam: Athenaeum, 1971.

West, M. L. *Greek Lyric Poetry*. Oxford: Oxford University Press, 2008.

Williams, Hector. "Secret Rites of Lesbos" *Archaeology* 47, no. 4 (1994): 35–40.

Williamson, Margaret. *Sappho's Immortal Daughters*. Cambridge, MA: Harvard University Press, 1995.

Winkler, John J. *The Constraints of Desire: The Anthropology of Sex and Gender in Ancient Greece*. New York: Routledge, 1990.

INDEX

Note: Italic page numbers refer to illustrations.

abortion, 66, 67–68
Acropolis, 19, 20
Adonis (god), 134, 146, 271n
Aegean Sea, map of, *xxv*
Aeschylus, 29, 63, 79
Aesop, 102
afterlife, 152–53
agapata (beloved), 60
aging. *See also* death and
    dying
  Cicero on, 150
  and dying process, 152–53
  lack of concept for middle
    age, 150
  and life expectancy of
    women, 149–50
  in Sappho's poetry, 155–58

women living beyond child-
    bearing years, 151
Alcaeus
  Aristotle on, 271n
  on Athenian calathos-
    psykter, *91*
  on *cherados*, 272n
  on emotion, 123
  exile of, 94
  on Hera, 261n
  and Pittacus, 92, 93, 95
  Pollux on, 275n
  religious poetry of, 145–46
  Sappho as contemporary of,
    xi, 6, 90
  wedding poetry of, 48
Alcman, 17–18, 44, 113

Alexander the Great, 45

Alyattes (king of Lydia), 6

Amphidromia ceremony, 3

amphorae, of Lesbos, 97–98

Anactoria, 260n

Anagora of Miletus, xi

Andromeda, 129, 266n, 270n

Andros, 23

Antimenidas, 90, 92

Anyte, 8, 10, 164–65

Aphrodite (goddess)

  and Adonis, 146–47, 271n

  in Sappho's poetry, 21,
    41–42, 47, 146, 273n

  Sappho's prayer of invoca-
    tion to, 140–42

  Sappho's prayer to, xix–xx,
    105, 116–17, 118, 119,
    138–40

  worship of, 134

Apollo (god), 43, 134, 135

Apollonius Dyscolus, xix,
  263–64n

Arabia, 97, 99

Archaic period, 7, 89

Archilochus, 7, 28–29, 111–13

Ares (god), 49

Argos, 163

Aristaenetus, 275n

Aristogiton, 87

Aristophanes, *Lysistrata*,
  18–19

Aristotle

  on aging women, 151

  on Alcaeus, 271n

  on childbirth, 73

  on Megacles, 90

  on pregnancy, 63, 64, 70

  women's age at marriage, 25

Artaxerxes (king of Persia), 89

Artemis (goddess)

  Athenian girls as "Bears" for,
    1, 20

  and childbirth, 72, 75

  relief of woman presenting
    infant girl to, 4

  Sappho's praise of, 4, 243n

  and transition to adult life,
    20–21

Arteus, 145, 146

Asclepiades, 112

Asclepius, 64, 69

Asia Minor, *xxv*, 6, 97, 98, 99,
  128, 134, 268n, 274n

Assyria, 97

Athena (goddess), 19–20, 87, 135, 139–40, 145

Athenaeus, 89, 98, 103, 266n, 267n, 268n, 270n, 271n, 272n

Athenian bowl showing mother and baby, 78

Athenian calathos-psykter with the Lesbian poets Alcaeus and Sappho, 91

Athenian cup showing mother and infant, 77

Athenian grave stele of young girl with doll and dog, 9

Athenian pyxis showing wedding procession, 41

Athens
  Amphidromia ceremony, 3–4
  children of, 1, 3–4
  comedies of, 167
  honoring women who died in childbirth, 74
  and Lesbos, xxii, 90, 92, 98
  religious practices of, 134, 135, 147

  rituals for girls, 18–21, 135
  sexual behavior of men in, 110–11, 112
  Thesmophoria festival in, 137
  women's lives in, xxii, 32, 51

Atthis (friend), xi, 128–29, 260n, 265n, 268n, 270n

Augustine, Saint, xxii

Augustus (Roman emperor), 166, 171, 257n

Babrius, 150

Babylon, 97

Bailers, 137

Baucis, 14–16, 163

Bearers of Secret Things, 19–20

el-Behnesa, Egypt, xi–xiv

Boeotian figurine showing mother and daughter, 77–78

Bronze Age, 7, 134

"The Brothers Poem", xxvii, 105–6, 237–38

Byzantine Empire, 171–72

Callias, 32

Camon (possible father), xi

Campbell, David A., *Greek Lyric I: Sappho and Alcaeus*, 173

Carson, Anne, 261n

Catullus, xxvii, 169, 262–63n

Cecrops (king of Athens), 19

Cercylas (husband), xi, 23, 33, 57

Cesarean sections, 74

Charaxus (brother)
  and Doricha, 88, 102–4, 108, 259n, 260n
  in Oxyrhynchus papyrus, 57, 88
  in Sappho's poetry, 5, 88–89, 99–102, 104, 105–7, 108, 259n
  in *Suda* encyclopedia, xi, 88

cherados (small stones), 272n

childbirth, 2, 25, 26, 70–75, 149, 151

children and childhood. *See also* family; marriage
  Amphidromia ceremony, 3–4

Athenian grave stele of young girl with doll and dog, *9*

daily life of, 8, 10, 14–16

education of, 10–13

gender differences during pregnancy and childbirth, 70, 71, 73

infants subjected to exposure, 2–3, 65, 74

men's relationship with, 77, 81

and mothers, 56, 62, 63, 76–83

naming of, 4

nursemaids caring for, 78–79

pets of, 8, 10

religious festivals for girls, 17–18

rites celebrating girls' puberty, 17–21

in Sappho's poetry, 10

survival of, 2

toys of, 8, 15, 16, 21

Cicero, 96, 150

Cleanactidae clan, 59, 92, 268n

Contra Costa County Library
San Pablo
5/6/2023 3:21:49 PM

- Patron Receipt -
- Charges -

ID: 21901025280334

Item: 31901056893151
Title: SEARCHING FOR SAPPHO
Call Number: 884.01 FREEMAN
Due Date: 5/27/2023

Account information, library hours,
and upcoming closures can be found
at https://ccclib.org/contact-us/,
or by calling 1-800-984-4636.

Cleis (daughter)
    birth of, 70
    name of, xi, 4, 57
    and Sappho's death, 159
    in Sappho's poetry, 24,
        58–62, 94–95, 99, 159,
        268n, 271n
    Sappho's relationship with,
        82–83, 155
Cleis (mother), xi, 4–5, 57,
    58, 95
coitus interruptus, 66
Constantinople, burning dur-
    ing Fourth Crusade, xx
Corinna, 162, 256n
Croesus of Lydia, 93
Cybele (goddess), 134
"The Cypris Poem", 238
Cyprus, 41–42, 63–64, 97,
    263n

dactyl, as unit of poetry, 13
Daniel, Robert, 156
Dante Alighieri, 118
death and dying
    dying process, 152–53
    funerals, 154–55

women's care of dead, 153–
    54
Demeter (goddess), 135–37
Demetrius, 30, 31, 49, 269n,
    270n, 273n
Diogenian, 272n
Dionysius of Halicarnassus,
    xx, xxvii, 47, 116–17, 257n
Dionysus (god), 135, 145, 146
divorce, 56, 64
Doricha, 88, 102–4, 108,
    259n, 260n

Echinos, Greece, 4
Ecrytos (possible father), xi
Eerigyios (possible father), xi
Egypt
    magic spells from, 114–15,
        119
    Sappho's experience of, 97
    in Sappho's poetry, 99
Eileithyia, 72
ekdosis (giving away), 38
ekthesis (putting aside), 2
Enheduanna, 242n
Eos (goddess), 130
Ephesus, 3

epithalamia (risqué songs), 48

Eresus, Lesbos, xi, 6, 89

Erigyius (brother), xi, 5, 57, 88–89

Erigyius (possible father), 243n

Erinna, *The Distaff*, 14–16, 163–64

Etarchos (possible father), xi

Eumenos (possible father), xi

Eunica of Salamis, xi

Euripides, 72

Eurycleia, 152

Eustathius, xxvii, 171–72, 263n

exposure, infants subjected to, 2–3, 65, 74

family
  bond between siblings, 86
  conflict between siblings, 87–88, 100–102
  conflict over money and inheritance, 87–88
  loyalty to, 85, 86–87

  political power of Sappho's family, xvii, 89

  Sappho's family in conflict with Cleanactidae, 59–60, 268n

  Sappho's family in conflict with Pittacus, 94–97, 108, 267n

  Sappho's family in Oxyrhynchus papyrus fragment, 57

  Sappho's family in *Suda* encyclopedia, xi, 57, 88, 243–44n

  in Sappho's poetry, 4–5, 100–102, 104, 105–8

  sons' support of widowed matrons, 151–52

  wealth of Sappho's family, xvii, 2, 8, 26, 33, 78, 99, 150

  women's relationships with brothers, 86, 87, 100–108, 162

Faulkner, William, 105

Fourth Crusade, xx

funerals, 154–55

Galen, 265n

Godward, John Williams, *In the Days of Sappho*, *170*

Gongyla of Colophon, xi, 261–62n, 268n

Gorgo, 261n, 262n, 272n

Greece
  Archaic period, 7
  Bronze Age kingdoms of, 7
  literary tradition of, 12
  map of, *xxv*
  poetry in, 7, 12–13
  trade networks of, 42, 98

Greek drinking cups, *hetairai* on, 55

Greek Linear B script, 134

Greek religion. *See also specific gods and goddesses*
  libation bowl with young women dancing around an altar, *143*
  modern beliefs compared to, 133
  mystery religions, 135, 153
  rites celebrating puberty, 17–21

and sacrifices, 134–35, 137, 154
  in Sappho's poetry, 130–31, 138–39, 142–44, 147, 272n
  Thesmophoria festival, 135–36, 137
  variety and complexity of, 134, 135

Greek vases
  bride's procession as theme on, 42
  childhood depicted on, 13, 16
  erotic paintings, 67
  mothers depicted on, 76–77
  ritual mourning by women on, 154
  rituals involving young women on, 20

Greek verse, forms of, 12–13

Grenfell, Bernard, xii–xv, *xiii*, xvii, xx, xxvii, 100, 106, 259n

Gronewald, Michael, 156

Gyrinno, 262n, 267n

Hades (god), 136

Harmodius, 87

Helen of Troy, 32, 51, 52–53, 262n

Hellenistic period, 164–66

Hephaestion, quotations of Sappho's poetry, xxvii, 45, 46–47, 60, 128, 129, 146, 265n

Hera (goddess)

in Alcaceus's poetry, 261n

in Alcman's poetry, 18

and childbirth, 71–72

in Homer, 46

in Sappho's poetry, 105–6, 107, 144–45, 146

worship of, 134, 145

and Zeus, 127, 131, 142, 144

Heraclitus, 10–11

Hermogenes, 270n

Herodian, 264n

Herodotus, 32, 103, 246n

Hesiod

on "beautiful ankles," 46

on childbirth, 71

on man's age at marriage, 24

poetry of, 7, 34

on woman's age at marriage, 25

Works and Days, 87

Hesychius, 274n

hetairai (prostitutes), 55

Himerius, 269n

Hipparchus, 87

Hippocrates, 26–27, 67, 113

Homer

and aegis as divine breast-plate, 267n

and children's education, 10–11

epic language of, 43

Erinna compared to, 164

and gods, 139

on Hera's "shining feet," 46

Horace on, 169

Iliad, xxvii, 7, 10, 38, 42, 51, 89, 90, 131, 171–72, 247n, 263n, 264n

on incantations, 119

lack of references to incense, 43

on Lesbos, 53

male perspective of, xxii

Odyssey, xxvii, 7, 10, 27, 31, 32, 33–34, 36–37, 51–53, 60, 79, 81–82, 108, 123, 139–40, 145, 146, 152–53, 261n, 268n
Sappho compared to, xviii, 13, 40, 43, 108, 130, 131, 140, 146, 264n
Sappho's knowledge of, 12
types of meter used by, 13, 40, 164
use of *agapata*, 60
homoeroticism. *See also* same-sex relationships
in Alcman's poetry, 17–18
in Sappho's poetry, 17, 120–28
Horace, xxvii, 107, 169–70
Hunt, Arthur, xii–xv, *xiii*, xvii, xx, xxvii, 100, 106, 259n
Hymenaeus (god), 49
Hyperides, 151
Hyrras, 90

Iadmon, 103
incense, in Sappho's poetry, 43

India, 97
Irwin, Eleanor, 124
Italy, 97

Jesus Christ, xiv–xv
Julian (Roman emperor), xxvii, 263n

Kikis, 90

Larichus (brother)
as cup bearer, 5, 89, 96
in Oxyrhynchus papyrus, 57, 88
and politics in Lesbos, 93, 96, 97
as Sappho's favorite brother, 5, 89
in Sappho's poetry, 88–89, 105–8
in *Suda* encyclopedia, xi
Laurentian Library, Florence, Italy, 141, 258n
Lesbos
and Athens, xxii, 90, 92, 98
coins featuring Sappho, xxvii

Lesbos (*continued*)
comedies featuring women
from, 167
Homer on, 53
Lydia as trading partner of,
32
map of, *xxv*
marriage customs of, 38–50
and Phocaea, 99
political history of, 89–90,
92–94
religious practices of, 134,
138, 145–46, 147, 261n
as Sappho's birthplace and
home, xvii, xxii, 6
in Sappho's poetry, 93–94,
98
trade network of, 42,
97–100
libation bowl with young
women dancing around
an altar, *143*
Library of Alexandria, xviii
Lobel, Edgar, *Poetarum Les-
biorum Fragmenta*, 173
Longinus, 120–21, 262n
love charms, 114–15, 119, 123

Lucian, 113
Lydia
Sappho's experience of, 6, 97
in Sappho's poetry, 32, 59,
60, 61, 99, 128, 129, 130,
260n
lyre, xviii, 13, 270n, 274n
lyric poetry, xi, 13

magic spells, 114–15, 119–20,
123
marriage. *See also* children and
childhood; family
Athenian pyxis showing
wedding procession, *41*
betrothal ceremony, 37, 38
Homer on, 36–37
marriage ceremony, 38–39
men's choice of potential
mate, 33–36
men's role in, 24–25, 26
and Sappho's wedding
songs, 29–30, 38–50, 122
women's choice in, 32–33, 36
women's marriage age,
25–27, 86, 151
women's role in, 25–27

Massalia, Gaul, 98–99
maternal mortality rate, 74
Maximus of Tyre
    Orations, 158–59
    quotations of Sappho's
        poetry, 265n
    on Sappho, xxvii, 260n,
        262n, 272n, 273n, 274n,
        275n
medical texts and practices
    on aging women, 151
    and pregnancy and child-
        birth, 62–70, 71, 74
    and sexual behavior, 111
Megacles, 90
Megara (friend), xi, 266n
Melanchros, 90
Menander, 37, 168
Menelaus, 145
men in classical world
    acceptable sexual behavior
        of, xxii–xxiii, 109, 110–
        12
    and birth of children,
        74–75
    education of boys, 10–11,
        12, 81

lack of responsibility for fer-
    tility, 64–65
marriage age for, 24–25, 26,
    151
and pederasty, 110–11
qualities of potential mate,
    33–36
relationship with children,
    77, 81
and women's religious prac-
    tices, 135–36
Mica (friend), 94
midwives, 71–73, 74, 75, 152
music, Sappho's training in, 13
Myrsilus, 92, 95, 96
Myrtis, 161–62
mystery religions, 135, 153
Mytilene, Lesbos, 6, 59,
    89–90, 92, 97, 98, 99

nature, in Sappho's poetry, 10
Naucratis, Egypt, 99–100, 103
Nebuchadnezzar (king of
    Babylon), 92
Nehemiah, 89
Neoboule, 28
Nossis, 165–66

Obbink, Dirk, 104–5
oracles, women as, 135
ostrakon (potsherd), Sappho's
    poetry preserved on, 140–
    41, 258n
Ovid, 5, 104, 169, 171, 260n
Oxford University, xii, 61,
    104–5, 173
Oxyrhynchus, Egypt
  Egyptian workers digging
    for papyrus fragments, *xiv*
  Grenfell and Hunt excavat-
    ing, xii–xv, xx, xxvii, 100,
    106, 259n
  papyri from excavation of,
    xii, xiii–xv, *xiv, xvi*, xvii,
    xx, xxvii, 57–58, 59, 61, 88,
    93–94, 128, 155–56

Page, Denys, *Poetarum Lesbio-
    rum Fragmenta*, 173
Panormus, Sicily, 96, 263n
papyri
  of Corinna's works, 162–63
  Egyptian workers digging
    for papyrus fragments at
    Oxyrhynchus, *xiv*

of Erinna's works, 164
  fragments from Milan and
    Copenhagen, 94–95
  in Oxyrhynchus excavation,
    xii, xiii–xv, *xiv, xvi*, xvii,
    xx, xxvii, 57–58, 59, 61, 88,
    93–94, 128, 155–56
  of Praxilla of Sicyon's works,
    163
  Sappho Poem 44, xv, *xvi*
    at University of Mississippi,
    105
Parian Marble, 95–96
partheneia (maiden songs), 17
patriarchal society, 31
pectis (type of lyre), Sappho's
    invention of, 13
Penthilidae clan, 90, 92,
    93–94, 267n
Persephone (goddess), 136,
    146–47, 270n
Perses, 87
pets, 8, 10
phallic humor, in Sappho's
    wedding songs, 50
Philo, 271n
Philostratus, 275n

Phocaea, 98–99

Phoenicia, 97

Photius, 274n

phratries (fraternal organizations), 4

Phrygia, 97

Phrynichus, 274n

Phrynon, 90

Pindar, 162, 169

Pittacus
  as ruler of Lesbos, 6, 90, 92, 93, 94, 95, 96–97, 108, 267n
  Sappho as contemporary of, xi, 6

Plato, 12, 25, 113, 168, 257n

plectrum (stick or quill), Sappho's invention of, xi, 13

Plutarch
  Advice on Marriage, 53–54
  on conception, 65
  and Myrtis's poetry, 162
  quotations of Sappho's poetry, 245n, 265–66n, 273n
  on sexual behavior of women, 113

Pollux, 265n, 269n, 274n, 275n

Pompeii, 112

Porphyry, 275n

Poseidon (god), 137

Posidippus, 3

Posippus, 103

Praxilla of Sicyon, 163

prostitutes
  in Nossis's poetry, 166
  Plutarch on, 54
  role of, 55–56, 76
  Sappho criticized as prostitute, xxi
  in Sappho's poetry, 5, 100–104, 108
  slave women used as, 66
  on vase paintings, 67

Psammethichus I (pharaoh), 99

Ptolemaeus, 81

Pyrrha, Lesbos, 92, 95

Pythia at Delphi, 135

Rhodopis. *See* Doricha

rhombos (bull-roarer), 123

Rome and Romans
  fall of Rome, xii
  and Sappho's influence on
    Latin verse, 166, 168–70,
    171

Salinger, J. D., *Raise High the
    Roof Beam, Carpenters*, 49,
    269n
same-sex relationships
  of men in classical world,
    110–11, 112
  in Sappho's poetry, 115–
    31
  and Sappho's prayer to
    Aphrodite, 116–17, 118,
    119, 138–39
  of women in classical world,
    112–19
Sapphic stanza, 13
Sappho of Lesbos
  on Athenian calathos-
    psykter, *91*
  biography contained on
    fragmentary papyrus,
    57–58, 88–89
  birth of, xvii, 6

childhood and youth of, 1,
    10, 11–12, 13, 14–17, 21
death of, 158–59
education of, 11–12, 13
family background of, xi,
    xvii, 2, 4–5, 8, 26, 33, 57,
    78
as first woman writer, xvii,
    241–42n
Grenfell and Hunt discov-
    ering papyrus fragment
    with poetry of, xv, xvii
identity of father, xi, 5, 243n
image of life, xxi–xxii, 161
legacy of, xxiv, 168–72
marriage of, 23–24, 26, 33,
    57
meaning of name, 243n
physical appearance of, xxi
quotations of ancient
    authors, xix–xx
recovery of works, xx–xxi
reputation of, xxi, 161, 172
sexuality of, xxii–xxiii, 23, 24
songs of, xvii, xviii
surviving remnants of
    poetry, xviii–xix, 242n

timeline, xxvii

translations of works, 172–74

types of poems written by, xvii–xviii

Sappho Poem 1, 174–75, 257–58n

Sappho Poem 2, 175–76, 258–59n

Sappho Poem 3, 176–77, 259n

Sappho Poem 4, 177, 259n

Sappho Poem 5, 177–78, 259n

Sappho Poem 6, 178, 259n

Sappho Poem 7, 178, 259n

Sappho Poem 8, 179, 260n

Sappho Poem 9, 179

Sappho Poem 12, 179

Sappho Poem 15, 179, 260n

Sappho Poem 16, 180–81, 260n

Sappho Poem 17, 181, 260–61n

Sappho Poem 18, 182, 261n

Sappho Poem 19, 182, 261n

Sappho Poem 20, 182–83, 261n

Sappho Poem 21, 183, 261n

Sappho Poem 22, 184, 261–62n

Sappho Poem 23, 184–85, 262n

Sappho Poem 24, 185

Sappho Poem 25, 186

Sappho Poem 26, 186

Sappho Poem 27, 186–87

Sappho Poem 29, 187, 262n

Sappho Poem 30, 188, 262n

Sappho Poem 31, 188–89, 262–63n, 273n

Sappho Poem 32, 189, 263n

Sappho Poem 33, 189

Sappho Poem 34, 190, 263n

Sappho Poem 35, 190, 263n

Sappho Poem 36, 190

Sappho Poem 37, 190, 263n

Sappho Poem 38, 191, 263–64n

Sappho Poem 39, 191

Sappho Poem 40, 191

Sappho Poem 41, 191

Sappho Poem 42, 191, 264n

Sappho Poem 43, 192

Sappho Poem 44
  papyrus fragment from
    Oxyrhynchus, Egypt, xv,
    xvi, 173
  translation of, 192–94, 264n
Sappho Poem 45, 194
Sappho Poem 46, 194, 264n
Sappho Poem 47, 194, 265n
Sappho Poem 48, 195
Sappho Poem 49, 195, 265n
Sappho Poem 50, 195, 265n
Sappho Poem 51, 195
Sappho Poem 52, 195
Sappho Poem 53, 196
Sappho Poem 54, 196, 265n
Sappho Poem 55, 196, 265–
    66n
Sappho Poem 56, 196
Sappho Poem 57, 197, 266n
Sappho Poem 58, 155–57,
    197–98, 261n
Sappho Poem 59, 198
Sappho Poem 60, 198
Sappho Poem 61, 199
Sappho Poem 62, 199
Sappho Poem 63, 199–200
Sappho Poem 64, 200

Sappho Poem 65, 200, 266n
Sappho Poem 67, 201
Sappho Poem 68, 201–2, 266n
Sappho Poem 69, 202
Sappho Poem 70, 202, 266n
Sappho Poem 71, 203, 267n
Sappho Poem 73, 203
Sappho Poem 74, 204
Sappho Poem 76, 204
Sappho Poem 78, 204–5
Sappho Poem 80, 205
Sappho Poem 81, 205, 267n
Sappho Poem 82, 205–6,
    267n
Sappho Poem 83, 206
Sappho Poem 84, 206
Sappho Poem 85, 206
Sappho Poem 86, 207, 267n
Sappho Poem 87, 207–8
Sappho Poem 88, 208–9
Sappho Poem 91, 209
Sappho Poem 92, 209
Sappho Poem 93, 210
Sappho Poem 94, 210–11,
    268n
Sappho Poem 95, 211–12,
    268n

Sappho Poem 96, 212–13, 268n

Sappho Poem 97, 213

Sappho Poem 98, 214–15, 268n

Sappho Poem 100, 215

Sappho Poem 101, 215, 268n

Sappho Poem 102, 215

Sappho Poem 103, 216–17, 269n

Sappho Poem 104, 218

Sappho Poem 105, 218, 269n

Sappho Poem 106, 219, 269n

Sappho Poem 107, 219

Sappho Poem 108, 219

Sappho Poem 109, 219

Sappho Poem 110, 219, 269n

Sappho Poem 111, 220, 269n

Sappho Poem 112, 220, 269n

Sappho Poem 113, 220

Sappho Poem 114, 221, 270n

Sappho Poem 115, 221

Sappho Poem 116, 221

Sappho Poem 117, 221

Sappho Poem 118, 222, 270n

Sappho Poem 119, 222

Sappho Poem 120, 222

Sappho Poem 121, 222

Sappho Poem 122, 222, 270n

Sappho Poem 123, 223

Sappho Poem 124, 223, 270n

Sappho Poem 125, 223, 270n

Sappho Poem 126, 223

Sappho Poem 127, 223

Sappho Poem 128, 224

Sappho Poem 129, 224

Sappho Poem 130, 224

Sappho Poem 131, 224, 270n

Sappho Poem 132, 225, 271n

Sappho Poem 133, 225, 271n

Sappho Poem 134, 225, 271n

Sappho Poem 135, 225, 271n

Sappho Poem 136, 226

Sappho Poem 137, 226, 271n

Sappho Poem 138, 226, 271n

Sappho Poem 139, 226, 271n

Sappho Poem 140, 227, 271n

Sappho Poem 141, 227, 271n

Sappho Poem 142, 227, 272n

Sappho Poem 143, 227

Sappho Poem 144, 228, 272n

Sappho Poem 145, 228, 272n

Sappho Poem 146, 228, 272n

Sappho Poem 147, 228

Sappho Poem 148, 228

Sappho Poem 149, 229

Sappho Poem 150, 229, 272n

Sappho Poem 151, 229

Sappho Poem 152, 229

Sappho Poem 153, 229

Sappho Poem 154, 230

Sappho Poem 155, 230, 273n

Sappho Poem 156, 230, 273n

Sappho Poem 157, 230

Sappho Poem 158, 230, 273n

Sappho Poem 159, 231, 273n

Sappho Poem 160, 231

Sappho Poem 161, 231

Sappho Poem 162, 231

Sappho Poem 163, 231

Sappho Poem 164, 232

Sappho Poem 165, 232, 273n

Sappho Poem 166, 232, 273n

Sappho Poem 167, 232

Sappho Poem 168, 232–33, 273–74n

Sappho Poem 169, 233

Sappho Poem 170, 233, 274n

Sappho Poem 171, 234, 274n

Sappho Poem 172, 234, 274n

Sappho Poem 173, 234

Sappho Poem 174, 234

Sappho Poem 175, 234

Sappho Poem 176, 234, 274n

Sappho Poem 177, 235, 274n

Sappho Poem 179, 235, 274n

Sappho Poem 180, 235, 274n

Sappho Poem 181, 235

Sappho Poem 182, 235

Sappho Poem 183, 235, 275n

Sappho Poem 184, 236

Sappho Poem 185, 236, 275n

Sappho Poem 186, 236, 275n

Sappho Poem 187, 236

Sappho Poem 188, 236, 275n

Sappho Poem 189, 236, 275n

Sappho Poem 190, 237

Sappho Poem 191, 237, 275n

Sappho Poem 192, 237, 275n

Sardis, Lydia, 128, 268n

Scamandronymos (possible father), xi, 5

Scythia, 97

Selene (goddess), 130

Semonides, 34–36

Semos (possible father), xi

Seres, 97

sexual behavior
    Archilochus on, 111–13
    Lucian on, 113–14
    male-centered active/passive
        model of, 110
    of men in classical world,
        xxii–xxiii, 109, 110–12
    socially accepted rules of,
        109–11
    of women in classical world,
        xxii–xxiii, 109, 112–14
sexuality. *See also* homoeroti-
    cism; same-sex relation-
    ships
    images from erotic vase
        paintings, 67
    of Sappho, xxii–xxiii, 23, 24
    in Sappho's poetry, 45–46
sexual preferences
    in classical world, 109–10,
        113–14
    modern categories of, xxii,
        109, 110
Sicily
    Sappho's exile in, xvii, 6, 60,
        61, 95–96, 155
    Sappho's experience of, 97

Simon (possible father), xi
Snyder, Jane McIntosh, 123
Socrates, 75, 107, 158–59,
    265n, 272n, 273n, 275n
Solon, 53–54
Sophocles, 86
Soranus, 66, 68, 71, 74
Sparta
    and Argos, 163
    childbirth practices in, 74
    and exposure of infants, 2
    marriage age for women,
        25
    religious festivals for girls
        in, 17
    religious practices of, 134
    role of women in, 11
    sexual behavior of women
        in, 113
spondee, as unit of poetry, 13
Stesichorus, xi
Stobaeus, 265n
Strabo, 103, 263n
Strato, 111
Suda encyclopedia
    on Atthis, 128–29, 260n
    on Gongyla, 261n

Suda encyclopedia (*continued*)
  on Sappho's family, xi, 57,
    88, 243–44n
  on Sappho's husband, 23, 57
Sulpicia, 166–67
Swinburne, Algernon Charles,
  158
Syracuse, Sicily, 96
Syrianus, 30

Telesilla of Argos, 163
Telesippa (friend), xi
Terentianus Maurus, 265n
Thales, 7
Thebes, 3, 134
Theognis, 111
Thesmophoria festival, 135–
  36, 137
Times Literary Supplement, 157
toys, 8, 15, 16, 21
Tryphon, 272n
Tyndareus, 32
Tzetzes, 172

University of Cologne, Ger-
  many, 156
University of Mississippi, 105

Verres (Roman governor), 96
Victorian scholars, 122, 124,
  126, 172
virginity
  death of virgin, 154
  flower as metaphor for, 29
  role of, 26, 27, 28–29, 87
  in Sappho's poetry, 27,
    29–31
Voigt, Eva-Marie, *Sappho et
  Alcaeus*, 173

weaving, 4, 11, 12, 45, 52, 76
wedding songs, of Sappho,
  29–30, 38–50, 122
West, M. L., 158
women in classical world. *See
  also* children and child-
  hood; family; marriage
  abortions, 66, 67–69
  acceptable sexual behavior
    of, xxii–xxiii, 109, 112–14
  bride's procession, *41*, 42–43
  care of dead, 153–54
  and childbirth, 2, 25, 26,
    70–75, 149, 151
  and divorce, 56, 64

duties of wife, 51–56, 63, 64–65, 76
education of girls, 11–12
everyday life in Athens, xxii, 32, 51
household management, 11, 25, 52, 53
infant girls, 2, 3, 4
knowledge passed among in private, 65
legal and social constraints on, 69
libation bowl with young women dancing around an altar, *143*
life expectancy of, 149–50
marriage age, 25–27, 86, 151
marriage choice of, 32–33, 36
as matrons, 151–52
midwives, 71–73, 74, 75, 152
as mothers, 25, 56, 62, 63, 74, 75–83
and mystery religions, 135
nursemaids, 78–79
as poets, 161–67, 242n

and politics, 96
and pregnancy, 62–70
prevention of pregnancy, 65–68
and procreation, 36, 55
relationship with brothers, 86, 87, 100–108, 162
relationship with mother-in-law, 79–80, 82
religious life of, 135–47
rites celebrating puberty, 17–21
same-sex relationships of, 112–19
and Sappho's childhood, 1
Sappho's poetry illustrating, xix, xxii, 1
slave women, 55, 66, 79, 102–3, 152
Thesmophoria festival, 135–36, 137, 138
virginity's role for, 26, 27, 28–31, 87
and weaving, 4, 11, 52, 76

Xanthes, 103
Xanthippe, 272n

Xenoclea, 80–81
Xenophon, 11, 55, 75

Zenobius, 273–74n
Zeus (god)
  Corinna's poetry on, 162–63
  creation of human beings,
    113

creation of women, 34,
  35–36
and Demeter, 136, 137
and Hera, 127, 131, 142,
  144
in Sappho's poetry, 105, 106,
  107, 273n
worship of, 134, 145